Theories of Human Nature

Theories of Human Nature

Joel J. Kupperman

Hackett Publishing Company, Inc.
Indianapolis/Cambridge

#569538105

For further information, please address
    Hackett Publishing Company, Inc.
    P.O. Box 44937
    Indianapolis, Indiana 46244-0937

    www.hackettpublishing.com

Cover design by Abigail Coyle
Interior design and composition by Elizabeth L. Wilson
Printed at Sheridan Books, Inc.

Library of Congress Cataloging-in-Publication Data

Kupperman, Joel.
    Theories of human nature / Joel J. Kupperman.
        p. cm.
    Includes bibliographical references and index.
    ISBN 978-1-60384-292-1 (pbk.) – ISBN 978-1-60384-293-8 (cloth)
    1. Philosophical anthropology–History. I. Title.
    BD450.K826 2010
    128.09–dc22   2010011504

The paper used in this publication meets the minimum requirements of
American National Standard for Information Sciences–Permanence of
Paper for Printed Library Materials, ANSI Z39.48–1984.

∞

Contents

Preface

This book is about two related subjects. One is the variety and range of accounts of human nature that have emerged in the last three thousand years. Almost all of these accounts are philosophical, and it is striking how many philosophers have embedded such accounts in their work. What also is striking (but not surprising, given the proclivities of philosophers) is that each of the accounts largely differs from the others.

The other subject is the very concept of "human nature," which is part of the basic set of ideas that most people have, including most people who have never studied philosophy. It provides an interesting case of commonsense thinking that turns out to enter the same territory as philosophy. Most of us sometimes say—of behavior that perhaps was not entirely predictable but is understandable—"That's just human nature." We all understand such remarks. But that does not mean that it is easy to put them in other words.

Philosophy often is concerned with meanings, and it does look like we often say things that have real meaning, even when we can't quite analyze what the meaning is. This can create puzzles. Does our familiarity with the idea of "human nature" mean that, at some deep level, we all are alike? Or does it mean something else, perhaps something more complicated?

All of this is by way of saying that what is contained in this book functions on two separate levels. Almost all of the book presents, and tries to make clear sense of, views of what would count as human nature. It describes and clarifies. The first two and the last chapters of the book though engage in what is sometimes called "meta-philosophy." They focus on what philosophers, and also the rest of us, mean when they talk about human nature (or about what amounts to human nature). This adds a reflective and analytic element to the description and clarification that constitutes almost all of the book.

One feature of philosophy especially should be mentioned. It is that philosophical examination rarely or never solves a problem by arriving at a truth so final that any further thought or discussion is pointless. Any genuine philosophical discussion therefore needs to be open ended in leading a reader or listener to think further and to craft her or his own perspective on what has been presented. Two features of this book are intended to promote this function of philosophy. One is that all but one chapter will be followed by two or three Questions for Further Consideration. These will point the reader toward unresolved issues that can be thought about. The other is that the chapters devoted to presenting a view or views of human nature (Chapters 3 through 14) also will be followed by a short list of Recommended Reading. Such reading will aid any reader in arriving at a broader view of what is presented in the chapter.

It is striking that most of the philosophers with whom this book deals did not analyze what could be meant by "human nature." One exception to this is Hannah Arendt, who flatly denied that she had a theory of human nature. It is clear that what she meant to deny was that she had any view that everyone shares the same nature. I will argue, though, that any view of what "human nature" is, that will cover the views of the other philosophers widely regarded as having a theory of human nature, also fits what Arendt says. She belongs in a book like this, along with such figures as Confucius, Aristotle, Hobbes, and Jean-Paul Sartre, none of whom maintained that we all have a nature that is entirely the same.

Let me thank Annalee Newitz, who first suggested to me that Hannah Arendt belonged in this book. I have many debts beyond this one. They include conversations with Karen Ordahl Kupperman, and with colleagues in my unusually collegial department at the University of Connecticut. Let me express my gratitude to the anonymous reviewers who made many very helpful suggestions. One of them, John Perry, is no longer anonymous.

There are debts also to Liz Wilson, for her judicious transformation of a manuscript into a book. The largest debt is to Deborah Wilkes, my editor at Hackett Publishing Company. She first suggested this book, and subsequently gave me a great deal of useful—sometimes very detailed—advice. It is often said that the era of thorough editing has passed and that the great editors have vanished. Deborah Wilkes has not vanished, though, and I am grateful.

Part I

INTRODUCTION

Chapter 1

Why Philosophers Have Wanted Theories of Human Nature

Human beings are not all the same, but there are situations in which we expect people generally to feel and do very similar things. This core of similarity leads to an idea of what we call human nature. There are more complicated ideas of what human beings tend to share, and we will be examining a number of them. However they vary, they all are concerned with what human beings tend to share, and they generally assume that there are certain things beyond this that humans tend not to share.

What is it that we often expect people to share? There are many views. Many great philosophers have developed theories of what it is that people generally tend to share.

This book will present a number of theories of human nature, almost all of them advanced by philosophers. It will examine each at some length. The reader may want to have some advance sense of the territory through which we will be moving. To this end, in this introductory section we will look at the variety of theories. Some of this will be illustrated by brief remarks about theories that later will be characterized more fully.

All, or almost all, of the theories that we will consider are far from negligible. Could they all be right? A theory can have "some truth," or be "largely right," without being the last word on its subject. This may turn out to be the case for some theories of human nature.

We can begin by asking why so many philosophers have wanted to have a theory of human nature. To ask this can help us to put our own ideas in perspective. But it also helps us to see how the idea of a shared human nature played a part in a variety of philosophical projects. The motivation and the context of theories can vary as much as do the theories themselves.

It should be added that philosophy, for almost all of its history, has overlapped with other areas of thought. A good deal of the work of David Hume in the eighteenth century and Friedrich Nietzsche in the nineteenth century, and also Confucius in ancient China, for example, could be regarded as psychology. One mark of philosophy, however, has been its preoccupation with comprehensive understanding of basic concepts and realities. Examples of basic concepts are those of knowledge, truth, goodness, and causation. Examples of basic realities are the usual characteristics of human life, and also the usual sources of human motivation.

Many general theories, of a variety of kinds, can be found in philosophy. We sometimes have moved toward a general theory of X because of genuine observation: we keep seeing Xs that are Ys, and it is appealing to suppose that the nature of X is that it is Y. One inducement, especially within the Western philosophical tradition, to look for a general pattern, is the idea (originally put forward by Socrates and by Plato) that to understand something is to find a timeless truth about it. This is to find its "form" or its essence, and normally leads to being able to provide a definition of the term for it.

The emphasis on knowledge of a very general kind, and on knowledge of whatever is unchanging, is not always dominant in Western philosophy, although it retains a strong appeal. It certainly has more influence in the history of Western philosophy than it has had, say, in Chinese philosophy. It has been commonplace among scholars of the leading schools of ancient Chinese philosophy to say that the most prominent movements give importance to processes of change and to how we might react to them. This is true of Confucianism, with its emphasis on civic responsibility, but even more true of Daoism, which recommends spontaneity and improvisation in life.[1]

All the same, three of the philosophical theories of human nature that will be considered in this book belong to Confucius and two later followers of Confucius. Something else must be involved here besides any ongoing urge to arrive at general theories. Even in Western philosophy, this must be true—especially if (as it seems) there is an especially strong impulse in the case of human nature to look for a theory.

Sources of Philosophical Theories of Human Nature

What makes it especially appealing to arrive at a theory of human nature? Let me suggest that different answers fit different cases. Further, for some philosophers it may be that arriving at a theory of human nature was the result of two or more factors rather than only one.

The three Chinese philosophers who are represented in this book certainly had sources of motivation different from those for most (although not all) of the Western philosophers represented. One of Confucius' central concerns, in his life and in his philosophy, was the possible transition (typically in someone's youth) from being an agreeable person who usually behaved fairly well to a more advanced and refined state of being a reliably good person. The goal was to be someone who had internalized, and also enjoyed, a life of virtuous action and harmonious human interaction. This is an underlying ethical concern, and it lends itself (in the Confucian tradition) to an emphasis on the things in us that would make possible such a transition.

Confucius' follower (more than a century after his death) Mengzi (Mencius) specifically identified the crucial element in us as a tendency toward benevolent impulses. Mengzi did not mean that we always behave benevolently. The benevolent impulse typically comes and goes, and it often is overridden by strong impulses of a selfish nature. Nevertheless, Mengzi argued that these occasional benevolent impulses showed that each of us had psychological tendencies that could be built upon in becoming consistently benevolent people. His later rival Xunzi had a somewhat bleaker view of what most of us are like; but he too thought that there were normal human tendencies that showed that a transition to genuine virtue was possible.

These are all cases in which an ethical judgment of how we could best conduct our lives influences a theory of human nature. Something like that is true both of the Indian philosophies to be discussed and of the Christian doctrine of original sin. The ancient *Upanishads* (which are fundamental texts of the tradition of philosophy associated with what became Hinduism) focused on an impersonal spiritual core (*atman*) of the self of any of us. This hardly implies that we are perfect or spiritual in our daily lives. But it is taken as pointing toward the possibility that we could transform our daily lives and liberate ourselves from the concerns of the world. This would require focusing on, especially in meditation, our *atman* and its ultimate identity with the divine nature of the universe.

Buddha's philosophy starts out by denying the existence of an *atman*. This yields a more complicated view than that of the *Upanishads* of what human beings are essentially like. It also leads to diagnosis of a basic human problem. Because we have the illusion of having a Self, and because we also then have desires, we inevitably will suffer.

Buddha's career was devoted first to finding, and then disseminating, a solution to this problem. Part of the cure is understanding his picture of what human beings are like. This facilitates clearing one's thought of the elements that lead to suffering. It also—to the extent to which reincarnation is meaningful—makes it possible for us to liberate ourselves from further reincarnation and instead to enter a diffuse and blissful state known as nirvana. A specific motivation, in other words, for the theory of human nature is the desire for effective therapy and also liberation.

Something like this is true of the Christian doctrine of original sin, as different as that is from Buddha's view. If a tendency to have occasional bad impulses is inherent in human nature, then every one of us must guard against it and also learn to be self-critical. Salvation remains a possibility, but moving toward it will be facilitated by an understanding of what the problem is. A general sense of our own limitations and needs matters. In a way, original sin is one side of a picture, the other side of which is grace.

All of these theories of human nature (Chinese, Indian, and that implicit in the Christian doctrine of original sin) are guided largely by a sense of human potential. This is less true (or not true at all) of many accounts in Western philosophies that place correspondingly more emphasis on what people are like even in an unfulfilled state.

The picture we get at the dawn of Western philosophy in Athens is (at least to a degree) different and more mixed. Plato and Aristotle had multiple sources for their theories of human nature. They both believed that good education can make possible a transition from being a sort-of-good person to being a thoroughly and reliably good person. In this they are a little like Confucius, although their ideas of what the right sorts of education are differ greatly. In addition, both Plato and Aristotle had what we nowadays would term extremely analytical minds. The running assumption was that to be a certain kind of thing was to have a certain nature, shared with everything else that fit the same general description. Human beings, as Aristotle said, are rational animals. Plato's analysis of the human soul had been that it had three parts, among which reason should dominate. This is not entirely the same as what Aristotle then said, but does point in the same general direction.

We can appreciate this better if we contrast the preoccupations of ancient Greek culture with those of recent Western thought. The ancient Greeks seemed to focus on the differences between humans (at least as they ought to be) and animals, whereas in recent Western thought more attention is paid to similarities (in our drives, needs, etc.). A striking example of the Greek preoccupation is found in the episode of Homer's *Odyssey* in which Ulysses and his crew land on the isle of the enchantress Circe. Circe with her potions turns the members of Ulysses' crew into animals but fails to turn Ulysses into one. In the end, he prevails on her to turn his crew back into human beings.

This can be read as a coded message that many humans (e.g., Ulysses' crew) are not far from being animals (and could slip back), but that the right kind of person (Ulysses) is not vulnerable to this. The question then is what makes human beings (especially someone like Ulysses) different from animals. Plato and Aristotle, centuries after Homer, both answered "reason."

A more complicated example of an expression of human excellence is to be found in a later passage in the *Odyssey*. This one concerns the Sirens, who were half women and half birds. Men's minds were overcome while hearing their song, so that they were swept away to destruction nearby. Approaching the area of the Sirens, Ulysses displayed not only rationality but also curiosity and the desire for a fuller range of experience. He saw to it that every member of the crew had his ears plugged with beeswax, so that none of them heard the Sirens' song. But he did not use the wax himself, and ordered the crew to tie him to the ship's mast, making it possible for him to hear the Sirens' song without any destructive consequences.[2] Aristotle might well have liked this passage. In his version of human nature, experience plays a major role in the rational functioning that is at the heart of human nature.

The eighteenth-century philosopher Immanuel Kant shared the view that reason is a central feature of human nature. The concerns that led him to this were not, however, entirely the same as Plato's and Aristotle's. They had more to do with the idea that reason is the element in human nature that grounds morality.

Views of human nature very different from Kant's had developed before him among British philosophers in the seventeenth and eighteenth centuries, most notably Thomas Hobbes, Bishop Joseph Butler, and David Hume. These philosophers were concerned with the real-world roots of social relations, including our restraint in interacting with other people and our respect for legal and political authority. Thomas Hobbes was a great pioneer in this, although both Butler and Hume then saw him as an extremist of sorts, who had developed a one-sided view of human nature.

Hobbes lived through the English civil war, in which the Puritans finally defeated and executed King Charles I and set up a parliamentary government led by Oliver Cromwell. To some extent, Hobbes experienced a society that had fallen apart. It was natural for him to attempt to analyze how societies, in more normal times, remain cohesive and functional.

Let me observe that this concern of Hobbes' now seems oddly topical. There certainly are (or recently have been) areas of the world in which once viable societies have fallen apart, leaving little effective law and order—and indeed rather little security in life. One might think of the former Yugoslavia (for a time), Rwanda, and Iraq. This certainly is not true of countries like Britain, Australia, and America. But, much as someone who is quite healthy must consider the possibility of becoming sick, we should keep our minds open to the idea that we may not be entirely immune to what has happened elsewhere.

As Hobbes saw it, the key to a viable society is a social contract. This is thought of as an agreement that has at least two components. One is a general commitment to a structure of laws and moral obligations. The other is a commitment to recognize the authority of a government, and of the person (e.g., a king) or persons (e.g., a government) in charge. Hobbes tried to be realistic about these commitments. He knew that they did not represent 100 percent compliance and that we still had to lock up our valuables and watch our purses and wallets. All the same, a viable society required that its members—by and large—were inclined to comply.

There are a number of further complications in Hobbes' account, which we can take up in Chapter 8. For the present, let us focus on the account of human nature that is embedded in Hobbes' philosophy. It is simply this: Each of us is, first and foremost, concerned with our own continued life and security and as much prosperity as can be achieved. We will go along with the social contract because, whatever deficiencies it may have, it gives us protection and security. There is no suggestion that regard for other people, or actually caring for some of them, plays any role in this. The dominant impulses in human nature are selfish and appetitive.

It is always tempting to regard competing philosophies as starkly and diametrically opposed to one another. This makes for a dramatic and simple picture. But in fact no major philosopher after Hobbes ever denied that there are selfish and appetitive elements in what we are like. Butler and Hume did differ from Hobbes in claiming that we needed a fuller and more nuanced picture of human nature.

Butler's position was that, just in terms of the construction of personal satisfaction, relations of caring for other people will generally contribute to (rather than subtract from) our lives. Altruism and self-interest often run in the same direction. This becomes especially clear if we factor in the satisfactions of harmonious relations with people we care for, who may well care for us. Fortunately, people tend to care for some others and to have some inclination toward harmonious relations with others. This was left out of Hobbes' account, but it is real.

This is a picture of human nature that does not exclude selfishness but does refuse to regard it as something that we should expect to be entirely and continuously dominant. Hume's view was similar but mainly addressed a different problem in Hobbes' account. Hobbes carefully had not claimed that there had been an actual event of humans gathering together to subscribe to a social contract. The claim rather was that if we examine the societies we live in, it is *as if* there had been such an actual agreement. The image, all the same, is of self-interested individuals agreeing on societal rules and structures. Hume pointed out that, even in primitive times, we have to think of families, small groups of people who care for each other. Once this emotional element is introduced into the picture, the notion that cooperative civic behavior is based on self-interest alone begins to look oversimple.

Hume also held (like Kant after him) that we can best understand morality if we see it as rooted in something in human nature. Hobbes had portrayed morality as one of the products of the self-interested deal represented by the social contract. Hume argued against this, asserting that morality rests on organized normal human sentiments of sympathy or benevolence. Hume's arguments that benevolence is an element of normal human nature are remarkably similar to those that had been offered more than two thousand years earlier by Mengzi (the Confucian philosopher referred to earlier in this chapter), even though it is not at all clear that Hume knew Mengzi's ideas.

One notion that Hobbes, Butler, Hume, and Kant all shared was that basically they regarded the construction of human society (whatever its roots were) as a success. Karl Marx represents a sharp dissent from this approach. He viewed human society as radically imperfect, in that it allowed for the persistent exploitation of ordinary workers and led to lives of "alienation" for large numbers of people. All of this motivated Marx's theory of human nature, in which changed social relations are a precondition for meaningful human lives.

The final two views of human nature on which we will concentrate are those of Jean-Paul Sartre, as found in his early work, and of Hannah Arendt. Both Sartre and Arendt were much more concerned with the development (and projection) of an individual nature than some of their predecessors had been. Sartre's concerns, in *Being and Nothingness,* are in part metaphysical. He argued that human beings are radically different, in being inherently incomplete in their natures, from ordinary physical objects. The incompleteness of an individual's nature is linked to the freedom (and the possibility of new developments) inherent in human life. Nevertheless we can freely construct patterns of life, even if these are always open to modification.

Arendt's inclusion in this study is a more complicated matter. She specifically denied that she had a theory of human nature. Nevertheless I will argue that, given one interpretation of what a theory of human nature is, she had one—and that it is interesting and important. She claimed that the revealing of a distinct nature (of a sort related to one's personality) is characteristic of human life. This amounts to an individualism we share, and could be argued to counterbalance the ongoing temptation to place most of the emphasis (in saying what we are like) on what we share with others, giving not so much attention then to individual characteristics.

The Idea in Everyday Life of Human Nature

Thus far we have been taking a first look at philosophers' accounts of human nature to be explored in this book. The guiding question here is, Why is the idea of a general theory of human nature so appealing? The general appeal of broad generalizations is often a factor, especially within the Western tradition. But there are other preoccupations—ethical, metaphysical, therapeutic, the attempt to explain morality, a wish for liberation, and so on—that are at work, depending on the philosopher.

Philosophers do vary in their underlying philosophical concerns. But they also interact with nonphilosophers and can be influenced by ideas "in the culture." There definitely are ideas of human nature at work in ordinary everyday conversation. Sometimes when people hear of someone's behavior in a crisis, or of someone's emotional responses, they will say, "That's only human nature." The idea seems to be that, while many or all of us have our peculiarities, there are many cases in which there is a generic human pattern to be found—and that what we do, think, or feel can be explained by reference to this pattern.

We need to look at this idea, in its various manifestations, in order better to assess the appeal (and also the limitations) of general conceptions of human nature. Here is a crude translation of "That's only human nature," as uttered in everyday conversation. It usually means that what X did or felt is pretty much what almost anyone would have done or felt in those circumstances, or in X's place.

There is a fine difference between "almost anyone" and "anyone." This is related to nuances and sometimes elasticity in the meanings of "generally" and "general." When something is said to be generally the case, this normally would be interpreted to mean that it is usually (but not always) the case. A general theory could be an account of what is always the case, or alternatively one of what is usually (or almost always) the case. The former is likely if it is a theory in the physical sciences. The latter may be more typical of theories in the human sciences.

But cases vary. Probably Plato's account of human nature—that humans have three parts to their souls, in which reason should dominate—is meant to apply (perhaps with some qualifications) to everyone. Aristotle's claim that man is the rational animal almost certainly would not have been applied to someone who was extremely mentally disabled. Both Mengzi and Hume were aware that there are individuals who seem to have no benevolent impulses whatsoever. But it is clear that Mengzi in particular held that humans generally—in the weak sense of "generally"—have a benevolent element and would not have claimed that all humans do. Hume's view comes close to this, with some qualifications that will be explored in Chapter 9.

Not only language, but also the real world, may turn out to be less neat than we might have liked. A modern discipline that looks at problems relevant to human nature is psychology. Psychological data often tell us how most people (maybe almost anyone) would behave in a certain sort of situation. It is rare though to find a claim that what people tend to do is what every single individual would do.

Here are two examples of studies that point toward conclusions about the behavior and thought of *almost* all people. A well-known and striking article by Kahneman and Tversky examined what we might expect to be the reactions to be of people who miss airline flights. To miss a flight is normally a reverse, whatever the circumstances. One might think that there would be about the same degree of regret in all cases. But Kahneman and Tversky found that almost all (but definitely not all) of the participants in their study expected that those who had narrowly missed flights would tend to be more upset than those who had missed a flight by a wide margin.[3] Plainly, they assumed that what their subjects expected was a good guide to what would be the case—yielding as reliable a judgment as could have been obtained by hanging around airports and talking to people who had missed their planes.

The other example is research on what is called "negativity bias." There is an interesting study of this by Rozin and Royzman.[4] To lose something—call it X—is usually regretted much more than a failure to get X. In a way, the two things might seem equal: they both involve being less well off by a factor of X than one might have liked. The difference though can be roughly accounted for by the idea of a baseline, a state treated as a basis for comparison and evaluation. If you already have X, your baseline for well-being includes X and you feel badly off without X. If you do not yet have X, your baseline does not yet include X; if then you fail to get X, you may well be disappointed but probably will not feel badly off in the way you would in the case in which you lose X.

There is nothing here though to suggest that everyone will react in the way that people in general tend to react. When we talk in everyday life about human nature, this makes most sense if it is not taken as referring to entirely shared patterns of behavior and of responses. A social science can yield valuable insights even if it is not precise in the ways in which, say, physics is, and even if the respects in which it is short of precision are softened (and also masked) by judicious use of statistics.[5] What counts as human nature, in this discourse, is the way in which almost anyone would tend (at least approximately) to behave and respond.

We will return to this discussion in the final chapter of this book, which will round out this book's account of theories of human nature. It also may help to provide a sense of what can be true in them.

Notes

1. For the theme of awareness of change in early Chinese philosophy, see for example Jane Geaney, *On the Epistemology of the Senses in Early Chinese Thought* (Honolulu: University of Hawaii Press, 2002).

Daoism will be discussed only very briefly in this book, in part because it resists having general theories, including general theories of human nature. Nevertheless the reader may want to know that Daoism did advocate a degree of responsiveness to the changing development of the world, and also placed great emphasis on the development of a personal spontaneity that was inconsistent with being guided by general rules. Discussion of the two major Daoist texts (*The Daodejing*, and the

Chuang-Tzu/Zhuangzi) can be found in my *Classic Asian Philosophy: A Guide to the Essential Texts,* 2nd ed. (New York: Oxford University Press, 2007).

With the exception of Confucius (Kongzi), whose westernized name is familiar, Chinese philosophers discussed in this book will be referred to primarily by their Chinese names. Hence it will be Mengzi rather than Mencius.

2. This inspired an especially clever example of graffiti, encountered some time ago in the philosophy section of the Cambridge University Library. A printed sign about fire alarms began "In Case of Sirens . . . ," below which someone had written, "Tie yourself to the mast."

3. Daniel Kahneman and Amos Tversky, "The Simulation Heuristic," in D. Kahneman, P. Slovic, and A. Tversky, eds., *Judgment Under Uncertainty: Heuristics and Biases* (New York: Cambridge University Press, 1982), pp. 201–208.

4. Paul Rozin and Edward B. Royzman, "Negativity Bias, Negativity Dominance, and Contagion," *Personality and Social Psychology Review* 5 (2001): 296–320.

5. For an exploratory discussion of related problems, see my "Precision in History," *Mind* 84 (1975): 374–389.

Questions for Further Consideration

1. Do we know that it is false that all human beings share the same human nature, and if we do, how do we know?

2. When we say of someone's behavior, "That's just human nature," does that say anything at all about that person's responsibility for the behavior?

Chapter 2

Two Foci of Theories of Human Nature

The previous chapter outlined a picture of what this book will be concerned with, though that picture is not exactly neat and simple. The theories of human nature that will be considered are quite diverse. Further the sources of these theories—which include the philosophical motivations that led to them—vary greatly.

We have, however, pointed to two poles in the territory of these theories. One is human nature as it generally is, even without improvements or refinements. The other is human nature as it ought to be. Some of the theories to be examined are at (or very near) one or the other of these poles. Other theories are, as it were, in the middle, including elements that point toward both poles.

This can be appreciated if we think more broadly of theories of the nature of something, where the something can be a nonhuman species, or a human or nonhuman organ, or a device or a kind of activity. Such theories can simply describe, as it were, the facts on the ground. The nature of an earthworm, for example, is likely to be stated in terms of the physiology, organization, and appearance of worms and of what they do.

However, an account of something can instead (or also) point to what the something is like when it is fulfilling its proper function, even though it may be different from this some of the time. A knife is an implement used for cutting. This is the nature of knives, even if there are some knives so blunt that they cannot cut anything. Similarly, the heart is an organ that circulates blood through the body. We might attempt to describe what hearts are by surveying how actual ones (say, human hearts) function. However, such a description would be complicated by the fact that things sometimes do not function quite as they should. Indeed, if the description included people who are dying (or have died) of heart attacks it would indeed be complicated. It also would run counter to the way we normally speak of the nature of an organ such as the heart.

It simply is the case that accounts of the nature of an organ (or device or activity) very often focus on what it is like when it is functioning as it should. That is its fulfilled nature. This—the end or the point of the organ, device, or activity—is usually what we are inquiring about when we ask questions about what an organ, device, or activity is or was. To ask, for example, of someone who has engaged in an activity, "What were you doing there?" is usually to inquire into the point of the activity, or what it was trying to achieve. To understand devices and organs, we want to know how they are supposed to function.

Given this, it is not difficult to see that some of the theories of human nature briefly characterized in Chapter 1 are concerned, at least in part, with human nature in a fulfilled state. Is man the rational animal, as Aristotle maintained? Certainly it is by and large true that people will be more clearly rational, at least at some moments, than dogs, cats, and chickens are. The contrast here between humans and other species on this planet in that respect is a fact.

However, many of us are sometimes irrational. Moreover, there are some unfortunate humans (the severely mentally disabled, for example), who do not clearly fall on the positive side of the contrast with other species on this planet. To speak of man as the rational animal, in short, is arguably only a half-truth with regard to some of us, and in a few cases does not seem true at all. It does point toward what humans are like when they are functioning at their best.

To return to the last chapter's brief outline of the theories of human nature that will be considered, we can see instances of focus on either or both of these two poles. The account of *atman* in the *Upanishads*, as the core of what anyone is, clearly is intended to point to a basic fact about anyone (or anything), whatever the actual functioning of that being or thing is. Recommendations as to the most desirable function of human life (as pursuing a meditative path toward the goal of thorough self-identification with *atman*) are in the background, but the basic claim has a matter-of-fact quality to it. The writers of the *Upanishads* regarded it as simply true that any accurate map of the universe (Brahman) would include a host of *atmans*, one of which has (as it were) your name on it.

Buddha's claim that any of us is a bundle of thought processes, and that there is no *atman*, has a similar matter-of-fact quality. It in effect challenges us to look within ourselves and find anything that seems impersonal, permanent, and unchanging. It predicts failure in finding such a thing. Beyond the factual claim, though, it too points toward recommendations of how to live. Because any "self" we have is a construction, woven out of the thoughts that we have had, there is no substantial thing-like self that we can identify within ourselves. Thus the boundaries between us and other people seem somewhat arbitrary and subject to chance: experiences or thoughts that they have had could easily have been ours. This opens the door to compassion and undermines any tendency to have desires for "me" (and ultimately to have desires at all).

The path to fulfillment is more strongly emphasized in the three Chinese philosophies to be considered, in that what is present in many or most or almost all people is characterized as the potential for true goodness. It is not entirely clear whether Confucius thought that almost everyone had the potential for refinement and ingrained goodness. But he clearly thought that the nature of many people, at some stage, points toward the potential for refinement and ingrained goodness. Confucius did not have much to say about what people are like in an earlier state, before they can activate their capacity of becoming refined and reliably good. There is a remark that, in that less-developed state, people are to some degree pretty much alike.[1]

Although Xunzi's account differs in its tone and details, it seems as if he would subscribe to this. He thought that we all begin life with natures that are crude and inadequate. If he had known about Thomas Hobbes' view (nearly two millennia later) that we are all self-interested and appetitive, he would have said, "Yes, we are like that at the start; but some of us develop beyond this and become civilized."

Mengzi (Mencius) is the clearest on this matter. Virtually everyone possesses the "germ of benevolence" in the form of occasional impulses that could be extended and become dominant in our lives. "Germ" (as in wheat germ) is an agricultural metaphor: there is something in us that can grow into real goodness. Mengzi's view was that possession of this germ of benevolence is simply a fact about human beings at an early stage of development. He admitted that there are occasionally people who do not seem to have even this germ of benevolence. But he said that they have lost it (which implies that they originally would have had it), and he even had a broad explanation (using the agricultural metaphor of what happens when there is overgrazing) of how this could have happened. As noted in the last chapter, David Hume shared Mengzi's view that people as a matter of fact sometimes have benevolent thoughts; he too said that what looks like an exception (e.g., the emperor Nero) is someone who lost his humanity.

The Christian doctrine of original sin, like the Indian philosophers just described and also Mengzi and Xunzi, points in two directions at once. It points toward a simple psychological fact: that there is universal human imperfection, so everyone has thoughts or occasional impulses of which they would be ashamed. Perhaps the claim goes beyond this in suggesting that everyone at least occasionally has behaved in a manner of which they would be ashamed. Even someone who does not accept the Christian framework might think that the doctrine supplies a plausible account of what human beings are generally like.

But the second-century Christian philosopher Tertullian (a pioneer of the idea of original sin) and others also want to say that realization that there is a sinful part of our nature should lead to positive steps. These would include repentance and regret, where appropriate. They also might well include a serious attempt to purify ourselves—not achieving perfection, but at least falling less short of it. An openness to God's grace could be part of this.

Thomas Hobbes' theory of human nature is definitely at the pole of describing existing facts. His tough, matter-of-fact approach does not point toward any recommendation of drastic refinement and improvement. It may be true that there *has been* some refinement. We, unlike our savage ancestors, have become habituated to adhering to the social contract. But basically, in Hobbes' view, we are the same sort of self-seeking, appetitive beings.

Bishop Joseph Butler and Hume, although they are united in rejecting Hobbes' account of human nature, did not have entirely the same foci. Butler held not only that we have some tendency to care for other people, but also that the satisfaction in our lives is likely to be significantly enhanced if caring relations are a major part. In short, Butler provided both an account of the basic facts of human nature as it widely exists and also one of what a fulfilled human nature would be like.

There are two elements in Hume's account that might seem to point toward a similar bipolar focus. In his *Enquiry Concerning the Principles of Morals,* he examined the case for holding that virtuous behavior is in our self-interest. This discussion centers on a character called the "sensible knave," who tries always to seem virtuous and will depart from virtue only when it looks likely that no one will know. Hume argued that this is a poor strategy in life, in large part because people tend to be very good at picking up on such tendencies—and hence won't treat the sensible knave as well as they would if he were genuinely virtuous.[2] This might seem like a recommendation for a form of human fulfillment. However, this particular fulfillment is already widespread in Hume's view; and any account of the facts of human nature as it now is would include the fact that a great many people already are to a large degree virtuous.

Hume also did consider the possibility that someone might wish to be a better person. In his essay "The Sceptic," he examined the difficulties and also the possibilities. On one hand, it seems clear that it is normally impossible to turn yourself into a different sort of person simply by an act of will. On the other hand, gradual progress toward such a goal is possible, particularly if the routines of life are adjusted along suitable lines. However, there is no indication in any of this of a particular view of what fulfilled human nature would be like.

Immanuel Kant's account of human nature centers on our possessing—above and beyond our largely self-interested inclinations—a faculty of reason that includes moral judgment. Kant here is like Hume in that any move toward a fulfilled human nature has already, in his view, largely taken place. Indeed Kant's modus operandi in all of his greatest works is to take forms of human thought that already have been developed and to analyze what their structure is and what truths are implied by the very nature of their functioning. In his *Critique of Pure Reason,* for example, he took it as given that we have knowledge of the world that includes judgments of cause and effect, and the use of mathematics in relation to the fabric of space and time. This nature of our thinking and experience is in effect embedded in the world that we know about, and because it comes from us we can have a priori knowledge of it. Kant similarly took it as given that human beings already have morality and that the implications of this are generally available in our thinking about how we should behave.

Karl Marx, in contrast, hardly thought that the vast majority of human beings have a fulfilled nature. His focus was on what such a fulfilled nature would be, with special attention to the inadequate character of the nature (and the life) that the vast majority of people have. This linked to a radical program of changing the nature of society and also of the patterns of human work. What most of us are now, in our lives, is from his point of view rather sad. Our lives are marked by alienation in human relations, in part brought about by class divisions, and also alienation in work that can be excessively specialized.

But this is hardly a theory of human nature. It is more like a diagnosis of a set of illnesses. Marx did have a theory of what constitutes fulfilled human nature that guides his call for change.

Finally, Jean-Paul Sartre and Hannah Arendt both had dramatic theories of human nature as it factually is. In Sartre's account we all are marked by an incompleteness (an element of "nothingness") in our natures, and thus are "condemned to be free." Sartre did have some ideas about how we can come to terms with this reality, but they are less prominent in *Being and Nothingness* than the diagnosis of our shared nature. The chief recommendation is honestly to accept our freedom and not to try to disguise it from ourselves.

Arendt, as I interpret her, saw that we all tend to reveal our distinctness—what we are like—in speech and behavior. This is treated as a basic fact. In this portion of her work, the basic fact is more prominent than any recommendations that can be connected with it.

All of these theories of human nature will be discussed in greater detail in the main parts of this book. However, it is important to realize in advance that they are disparate, not only in their philosophical motivations but also in whether the "human nature" they focus on is human nature in its raw, most basic form, or fulfilled human nature, or both. There is sometimes a tendency among both writers and readers of philosophy to assume that competing philosophers, however they may disagree, are asking the same questions. It should be clear though that great philosophers who have put forward theories of human nature are *not all* asking the same questions.

Notes

1. See *Confucius, Analects,* trans. Edward Slingerland (Indianapolis: Hackett Publishing Co., 2003), 17.2, p. 200. All further references to the *Analects* will be to this edition. The reader with a different translation should be aware that the number of a passage can vary slightly from one translation to another.

2. See *Enquiry Concerning the Principles of Morals,* ed. J. B. Schneewind (Indianapolis: Hackett Publishing Co., 1983), Section IX, Part II, p. 81.

See also Paul Ekman and E. L. Rosenberg, *What the Face Reveals,* 2nd ed. (New York: Oxford University Press, 2004) for an illuminating account of momentary "micro-expressions," which can influence our impressions of people even if they are too brief to be consciously registered. This provides an empirical basis for some of what Hume claimed to be the risks of being a "sensible knave."

Questions for Further Consideration

1. Can we say that having some capacity or potential is part of someone's human nature, even if that person is not manifesting that capacity or potential in any way?

2. Are there basic capacities that we can say are part of almost everyone's nature?

Part II

SOME ANCIENT
VIEWS OF
HUMAN NATURE

Chapter 3

The *Upanishads* and Buddha

This chapter and the next examine the oldest major theories of human nature. Some of the principal *Upanishads* appeared in India as early as the eighth or seventh centuries BCE.[1] Buddha and also Confucius (Kongzi) were born roughly midway through the sixth century BCE. Together these two chapters give much of the foundations of philosophical thought in India and in China.

One might begin an investigation of human nature by supposing that there could be some personal characteristics that are shared by all human beings. This would leave open the possibility that human beings usually or always have some qualities that are distinctive and individual, so that more is true of a person than could be specified in terms of the shared human nature. In the end you might describe someone by (a) saying what his or her social class, age, occupation, general appearance, and so on are and (b) saying as well that, of course, the person also has the normal qualities that are part of shared human nature.

Things like social class, age, and such characteristics are usually not difficult to determine. The interesting and difficult question is "What is it, if anything, that all (or almost all) human beings share?" The *Upanishads* center on a subtle and ingenious answer to this question, along with recommendations for the kind of life that (given the answer) seems desirable. As we shall see in the latter part of this chapter, Buddha then built a philosophy on his rejection of the answer given in the

Upanishads. He too then had recommendations that stemmed from his view of human nature.

Might human beings all share a common nature in some of the ways in which they think and act? Here is one reason why this might seem implausible. Typically a person does not even entirely share a nature with himself or herself as of a year or two ago. People constantly are changing in various ways. The changes may be very small and incremental, and perhaps notice-able only when they have reached a cumulative state. All the same, even very slight changes represent differences.

One of the sayings of the Greek philosopher Heraclitus (c.500 BCE) was that you could not step in the same river twice. Different water would be coming through; the banks might have shifted a fraction of an inch or more, and one can imagine other changes as being likely. In much this spirit, Heraclitus might have said that you can't meet the same person twice.

With this in mind, we have reached a point that philosophi-cal thought often comes to: where there are two opposing views, each of which seems highly plausible and attractive. On one hand, people do change. That is undeniable. People will never be entirely the same even from one day to the next. On the other hand, we also have a strong sense that we are the same person as we were last week or last year. It seems hard to go against that.

Indeed there is a case for positing genuine awareness of our identity through time. The philosopher Sidney Shoemaker uses the example of knowing that it was I that broke the front window yesterday.[2] One might think that we know this simply on the basis of memory. But Shoemaker points out that what we remember, strictly speaking, is that somebody broke the front window yesterday. Knowing that this person was you is a further step, and is not given by memory.[3]

Let us assume for the sake of argument that there is a sense in which you really are the same person through periods of time. Bear in mind that a shared human nature does not include every-thing that is true of all persons. Even if there is a shared human nature, it surely cannot include everything about persons: we all have our little idiosyncrasies and quirks, and also distinctive personalities. This suggests then that an entirely shared human nature would *not* include personalities, or any of the features of thought or behavior that reflect personality, or for that matter the content of personal experience.

What is left that can constitute a shared human nature, one that we can share with others and also with what we were at other times? The answer of the *Upanishads* is that—beneath personality and other individual characteristics—there is an entirely impersonal region of the self. Because it is impersonal, it never changes; and because it is impersonal (lacking anything connected with individual identity), it is shared with other people (and also with other beings). This impersonal core of the self is called *atman*.

This is a distinctive view, and some readers may not find it immediately compelling. But it is worth noticing that it does lend itself to a sense that you can be (and can be aware of being) the same person that you were a year or two ago, and the same person as you will be in the future.

The *Upanishads* hold that through meditation you can gain contact with your *atman* and be aware of its persistence. There are other ramifications, and to explore these we need to look at the religion of India during this very early period. First, two things should be said about the relation between philosophy and religion. They are usually in Western culture thought to be distinct. One ground of the distinction is that philosophies typically argue, either explicitly or at least implicitly, for their conclusions, whereas the claims made by religions often are regarded as a matter of faith. The Bible and the Koran, for example, do not argue for what they assert, but do appeal to faith. They are clearly on the religion side of the divide.

However, there are some texts that are argued but also do have clear religious implications. The writings of Maimonides, Thomas Aquinas, Ibn al-Arabi, and John Calvin offer this combination of features. So do the *Upanishads*.

In the background of the *Upanishads* is a religious tradition in India that in many respects was like the religion of Greece at the same time. There were many gods and goddesses, each with distinctive functions. Like the ancient Greeks, the inhabitants of India believed in reincarnation. In the Greek version, the dead drink from the river Lethe (forgetfulness) before they go on to new lives. Plato ends his *Republic* with the Myth of Er, who supposedly had an after-death experience in which he witnessed the souls of the dead choosing new lives.

The ancient Indian version emphasized the way in which one's status in the next life corresponds to the degree of one's virtue in this one. The law of Karma characterizes an automatic process in which virtuous people rise to a higher caste in their next lives. Someone who had not been virtuous would move down in the caste system, or be reborn as, say, a frog.

Religions, like rivers and persons, change. In some places in the first millennium BCE there was a move from a religion of many gods and goddesses to a religion of a single god. In ancient Persia, for example, Zoroaster pioneered the idea that the gods and goddesses that had been worshipped did exist but in fact were evil spirits. There was only one god. In ancient India an idea developed that all of the seemingly distinct gods and goddesses were really aspects of a single divine reality—which comprised the entire universe. This spiritualized universe was known as Brahman. In religious terms this amounted to a subtle form of monotheism. (*Really,* there was only one divine reality). In its central claim about the universe as divine, this anticipated the seventeenth-century philosopher Spinoza's view of the relation between God and the universe.

We have seen that the *Upanishads* developed the view that everyone has an impersonal core of self, referred to as *atman*. Because this core of self is impersonal, it is easy to suppose that everyone's *atman* is qualitatively the same. This would be true not only of the *atmans* of humans and animals but also of the *atmans* of the traditional gods and goddesses. This led to the view that everyone and everything (including the traditional gods and goddesses) is identical with Brahman. The identity would be like the way in which a drop of ocean water is part of, and the same stuff as, the ocean, even though of course the drop (unlike the ocean) is not thousands of miles wide. Our identity with Brahman hardly means that we share the features of Brahman that amount to divine status.[4]

If *atman* represents a shared human nature, some questions still remain. A reader may think that this early Indian view is a nice story—and does center on a claimed something in us that is impervious to change, and plausibly could be regarded as characteristic of all humans. But what reason do we have to think that there is an *atman?* The fact that it is a philosophically convenient idea might not look like an argument for its reality.

Clearly, an impersonal spiritual reality deep within us is not part of the everyday experience (or even the occasional experience) of most of us. But then some things that are real turn out to be very difficult to experience and perhaps can be experienced only in indirect or unusual ways. This would apply to, say, our experience of neutrons, even though we all know that neutrons are real.

What does not occur every day still might occur in some special forms of experience. One possibility is what would be termed mystical experience, which looms large in a number of religious traditions. The idea is that some people, as a result of extraordinary efforts or receptiveness, can have revelatory episodes that are not available to most of us. These experiences typically are quite difficult to put in words, because they go beyond familiar categories. Often it is said that they are impossible to put in words, but this may be an exaggerated claim. Mystics sometimes write books. Against this background, we need to look at the possibilities of experience of *atman.*

Being in Touch with Your Atman

It is clear that the writers of the *Upanishads* believed that some people do have experience of their *atmans,* and they probably believed that many of us (if we had the right discipline and commitment) could also have such experience. They also believed though that a great deal of time and work on oneself would be required to have such experience. Further, the experience would have to be of a special character. It would have to be non-dual.

To appreciate the term *non-dual* one needs perspective on examinations of one's self. Most of us tend to think not only that we are, in some sense, the same person throughout our lives, but also that we have within ourselves what might be termed a "substantial self"—a real me—which is what remains the same throughout life (and afterward in any paradise or hell).

The eighteenth-century philosopher Bishop Butler (whose view of human nature will be presented in Chapter 9) distinguished between two views of how one could remain the "same" person. One was "strict and philosophical"; the other was "loose and popular." Butler opted for a strict and philosophical view. This implied that we have substantial thing-like selves, which remain in place throughout our lives.

A natural response would be to look introspectively for a substantial self, checking your consciousness at various times to see whether there was one that was present and remained in place. David Hume tried this, and came up with a negative answer. As we will shortly see, Buddha (more than two millennia before Hume) also came up with a negative answer.

Both Hume and Buddha's followers did believe that there is a conventional respect (corresponding to Butler's loose and popular sense of same) in which we remain the same person throughout our lives. There is after all a continuity in bodily appearance, some patterns of thought that more or less persist, and also memories that connect some moments of our lives with previous moments. (The memories, as already noted, do not prove that we are the same. But they can make it highly plausible that we are the same.) Hume and Buddha's followers were convinced that, although there is a loose conventional sense in which we remain the same person, there is no substantial self (a "me") within us that remains the same. Buddha put this in terms that opposed the *Upanishads:* there is no *atman* to be found.

This negative view of *atman*'s reality may seem very persuasive. But it is open to objections. Here is one. If Hume (and before him Buddha) looked for the self and could not find it, what was doing the looking? It is hard not to think that Hume's self was doing the looking for his self. This seems bizarre, and it also suggests that there might be a contradiction within the negative position.

The writers of the *Upanishads,* who were among other things sophisticated philosophers, anticipated this wrinkle. That is why they insisted that the experience of *atman* would have to be non-dual. What non-dual means in this context is that the experience of *atman,* unlike ordinary experiences, would *not* involve a separation between subject and object (in which the subject is looking for or at the object). If the subject and the object are the same, the experience would not have the polarity of ordinary experience and would not be experienced as an experience *of atman.*

Clearly this makes the relevant experience not only hard to have but also hard to talk about. Let me attempt a reconstruction. If somehow one managed (after much preparation) to have an *atman*-experience, it could not be—at the time of the experience—put into words. To put it into words would be to sink back immediately into a subject-object dichotomy. The experience would be like a silent immersion in a reality that was blank but also a source of peacefulness and joy. After this immersion, one would come out of the state and might well reenter the world of subject-object pronouncements. Then one could say that one had had an *atman*-experience.

The immersion in *atman* would occur during meditation. We need to examine the kind of life that might center on this and what its rewards could be. First though, let me make two remarks about meditation. One is that meditation, especially in this case, is something that requires preparation and also stage management. If someone, walking near New York's Times Square in a normal manner, suddenly said, "I will pause and meditate now," that would be a recipe for failure. There would be too many distractions, and in many ways the effort would be unnatural. Those schools of thought that encourage meditation usually recommend strongly that it occur in quiet surroundings without other people being around.

Beyond that, it is well known that the human mind tends to wander, something that definitely would spoil any meditation.

There has to be training in steadiness and concentration. In the world in which the *Upanishads* became a major guide, this was held to require techniques (the word for which was *yoga*), which needed to be gradually mastered.

Too much food might contribute to excess energy and restlessness. Therefore it was advisable to eat very little. There are legends of Buddha's early life, in which he consorted with Hindu mystics who were attempting to follow the path recommended by the *Upanishads*. They and he ate extremely little food. This was fine for the purposes of Buddha's companions, who were looking as it were for a private salvation. Buddha, however, was looking for a message that he could communicate to people threatened with lives of suffering—a message that would teach them how to avoid suffering.

He decided finally that he would be unable to arrive at this message unless he had food energy and returning strength. So he left his companions and had a good meal. Later he formulated his "Middle Way," which includes the thought that it is best not to eat too much or too little.

The meditation recommended by the *Upanishads* required considerable discipline and concentration, but also that there be very little food energy. Many readers might suppose that meditation has a general nature, so that meditation connected with various philosophies or cultures will have a common form: that in all of them you sit quietly and things happen in the mind. The reality of forms of meditation turns out to be more complicated than this. In particular, the meditation favored by Buddha's immediate followers was quite different from that associated with the *Upanishads*. Buddhist meditation, in its early forms, was designed to bring home unwelcome truths, such as the realities of illness and loss, aging, and death. A favored mode in some places involved sitting in a charnel area, where there were skulls and other parts of human remains, and meditating while viewing these.

The meditations associated with the *Upanishads* in contrast did not require focusing on particular things but rather involved emptying the mind and in particular eliminating boundaries within experience. To take seriously the claim that *atman* is Brahman would be to realize that any boundaries in the world have only a superficial reality. The deep reality is that everything partakes of the same substance.

Let me expand on this point. Once someone takes in the idea that there is an impersonal *atman* within you that is identical with Brahman, that person will have what might be termed a split-screen image of reality. The world can be seen as Brahman, a qualitatively unified field of *atmans*. But it also will be seen as a conglomeration of people and things. The people in this image will be differentiated in a number of ways: by gender, caste, age, and so on, and also by how far they have gone in realizing their oneness with Brahman. But in the image of the world as Brahman, they will be all the same.

How can people hold two such disparate versions of reality? Could both of them be in some sense true? The text of the *Upanishads* moves effortlessly from one version to the other. Everything is Brahman, but there is concern for how an individual can come fully to realize this. Can this make sense?

There is one classic discussion of two views of reality that I have found helpful in coming to terms with the *Upanishads'* split-screen image. It is a famous talk by the astronomer and philosopher Arthur Eddington, in which he spoke of "two tables" in front of him. Really, in normal terms, there was one. But his point was that—looking at that table—you could speak (from the point of view of ordinary experience) of a table that was dense and solid, and you also could speak (from the point of view of nuclear physics) of a table that was largely empty, with microparticles whizzing through it.

Whether or not one wants to speak of "two tables," there are two disparate sets of truths about the table in front of Eddington. This seems to me a good model for an understanding of the two views of reality that the *Upanishads* move between. Here is a further similarity. Eddington clearly thought not only that both the ordinary account of the table and the account derived from nuclear physics were true, but also that the nuclear physics account was the deeper truth. In much this way the *Upanishads* clearly hold that the view of the world as Brahman is a deeper truth than the view of the world in which there are differences among individual people and things of a wide variety of sorts. It might be helpful, in grasping their view, to think of the world as Brahman as ultimate reality, and the world as a conglomeration of individuals as superficial reality.

In terms of the individual, and his or her fulfillment, the transition between views of reality was crucial. Occasional experiences of being in touch with *atman* were a good first step, but the ideal was to reach the point at which one's ongoing view of the world was dominated by the sense of the world as Brahman. This would lead to liberation. After death, instead of being reincarnated (which may have been thought of as wearisome, after so many times) one would enter a highly positive state called *moksha*. This would be a state of being that was different from any previously experienced, although less different from dreamless sleep than from waking experience or from dreaming. The state would be undifferentiated: there would be no "consciousness" in the sense of subject-object experience.

In the light of all this, we can summarize the *Upanishads'* view of human nature as follows. The shared nature of human beings, including those leading ordinary lives, is that deep within themselves they have an impersonal spiritual nature, an *atman*. Most people are entirely or largely ignorant of this. The fulfilled nature of human beings is to have realized fully, in an ongoing way, that the deepest truth about them is that they are an *atman* identical with Brahman.

As we will see shortly, Buddha's views both of the shared nature of people leading ordinary lives and of what fulfilled human nature would be are different from these. Buddha's philosophy is like that of the *Upanishads* in the order of elements in his views. At the foundation is a claim about features of human nature in, so to speak, its wild (or unenlightened) state. Some of these features would not persist in enlightened humans. Recommendations for how to become enlightened are keyed to recognition of the basic truths of initial human nature. Finally there is a characterization of what it would be like to have become enlightened, which provides a representation of fulfilled human nature.

Buddha's View of Basic Human Nature

The most basic claim is that there is no *atman*. What we are fundamentally like (whether we are unenlightened or enlightened) is outlined in the opening line of the *Dhammapada:* "All that we are is the result of what we have thought: it is founded on our thoughts, it is made up of our thoughts." This refers, as quickly becomes clear, to the consequences of having certain thoughts. But it also is meant to be taken literally. What we introspectively encounter within ourselves are thoughts, especially interwoven thoughts and patterns and tendencies of thought. That is all there is: there is no deeper reality underlying them.

In this respect Buddha's view is rather like the one that David Hume developed more than two thousand years later, speaking of "bundles" of thoughts and other psychological occurrences as playing some of the role that people like Bishop Butler had wished to assign to a substantial self. At this point the two accounts diverge. Hume was deeply involved in philosophical psychology and devoted much of Book II of his *Treatise of Human Nature* to an account of how we develop the personal selves (the characters) that we have. Social relations and the influence of "mirroring fellow minds" figure significantly in this. Buddha's concern was not so much this (although he did develop an interesting philosophical psychology) as it was with therapy. As he saw it, normal human life is shot through with suffering, and this suffering is inevitable *unless* one can get beyond the mind-set that the vast majority of people share. The first step in this is to realize that there is no *atman* and that one is essentially an interwoven connection of thoughts, patterns of thoughts, and so on.

At the center of his diagnosis of the human condition is the claim that human beings normally are full of desire. Bear in mind that "desire," in its traditional sense, refers to a strong preference, such that if we do not get what we desire this will bother us considerably. Desire in short involves "attachment" to some thing or things: either to the things themselves, or at least to the idea of the things. Either way, if we fail to get what we desire, the mark of our attachment is that it will be a very negative experience for us.

There are many things, experiences, or relationships that we very much would like to have, or would very much like not to lose out on or miss. These are objects of desire. There are some things or experiences on the other hand that we would like to have that do not matter so much to us. If we miss out on them or lose them, we can honestly say that it is "no big deal." These represent mild preferences and not (in the traditional meaning of the word) desires. If all of our preferences were mild, Buddha thought that we would be immune to suffering.

It seems clearly true that human beings, from their first cry as babies onward, tend to be full of desires and therefore vulnerable to suffering. This is as a matter of fact normal human nature. Buddha, like the authors of the *Upanishads* (but in different respects, and for different reasons), thought that normal human nature is faulty and can be improved on.

Why do we tend to be full of desires? Buddha thought that a major factor is the widespread impression that there is a "me" in each of us, a substantial self that has needs. If we can think of ourselves as a bundle of psychic elements, that would lend itself to taking ourselves (and our alleged needs) less seriously. This is particularly the case if we realize that the experiences or outcomes (good or bad) that constitute our lives (and what we are) could easily have been someone else's. This awareness not only can make us more detached about our preferences but also should encourage our compassion for others whose experiences and outcomes turned out to be unappealing.

Buddhist compassion, it should be noted, would have to be a set of mild preferences for the well-being of others. Benign desires are, all the same, desires. One would want others not to suffer, and presumably would do what one could to help them avoid suffering. But someone who was helpful and kind in this way would not be, if she or he had achieved the loss of desires, seriously disturbed if things went wrong. To be seriously upset would show that one had not lost all of one's desires.

Thoroughly purifying the mind of desires would have rewards. The calm that it would involve might, among other things, enable a person to be more effective in compassionate activities. The most obvious reward—given the logic of suffering—would be immunity to suffering. It also is claimed that someone who achieved this would experience bliss. This was thought of as a natural result of calming the mind and emptying it of attachments and desires. All of this was part of Buddha's image of what fulfilled human nature would be like.

A final reward would be that someone who achieved thorough purification would avoid further reincarnation and could enter a permanent blissful state called *nirvana*. There are complications surrounding this reward though that need to be explained. It is not a simple story.

First, Buddha tended to be noncommittal about the afterlife. Very little is said about nirvana. There is at least one Buddhist text in which Buddha claimed to have reached nirvana while still alive. So it is not clear whether nirvana is always something that one enters only after death.

Secondly, in the history of Buddhism more than one view developed of whether enlightenment meant entry into nirvana. The history of Buddhism, like the history of some other major religions, was marked by schisms and also a growing popularization of some of the central ideas.

In Buddhism's case, it looks as if the original movement was at least as much a philosophy as a religious movement. Buddha was clear that he was a human being who had discovered an important and useful truth about life: there was no early suggestion that he was a god or that he should be worshipped. Later on, statues of Buddha proliferated, and many venerated him in almost the way in which they would venerate a supernatural being.

The first major schism developed in relation to the early Buddhist idea that any individual could perfect himself or herself, eliminating all desires. The monk Mahadeva alleged, among other things, that there was physical evidence that monks had lustful thoughts while asleep. This suggested that one would not be able to become liberated without help. It is a short step from this to the idea, important in some of the Northern (Mahayana) schools of Buddhism, of the bodhisattva—a celestial being that has achieved enlightenment and could enter nirvana but postpones this in order to help us in becoming liberated.

In some forms of later Buddhism there also was a shift in the treatment of reincarnation. Reincarnation had been treated in the *Upanishads* as a fact: the *atman* of someone who had not been liberated would go on to a new life. Plainly it cannot be that simple if there is no *atman* to travel from one life to the next. If Bloggs, who has a bundle of thoughts (and some characteristic ways of responding to the world) dies, will his bundle of thoughts and characteristic ways of responding to the world go on to a new life? And if they do, do we consider the new person to be Bloggs in a new incarnation?

Some early Buddhist texts allow that patterns of thought (including that of having desires) can have a causal role in the formation of a new life. The question of whether the new life then is a reincarnation of the old life is treated as *not* having an unproblematic answer. In an early classic, *The Questions of King Milinda,* the king asks the Buddhist teacher Nagasena, "He who is born, Nagasena, does he remain the same or become another?" Nagasena answers, "Neither the same nor another." To explain this answer he begins by suggesting some of the complications of identity questions, including the question of whether—when a lamp burns all night—its flame at the beginning of the night is the same as its flame at the end of the night. (One might also ask whether, if the flame of one lamp is used to light another lamp, the flame on the second lamp is the same as the flame on the first.) By our normal criteria of what counts as "the same" or "not the same," these questions do not have a clear answer of yes or no.

In some, although by no means all, of the later forms of Buddhism, reincarnation was in contrast treated as unproblematic. The idea was deeply embedded in popular culture, and some schools of Buddhist thought simply accepted it. Its resonance in the wider culture had some striking manifestations. As we all know, Western novels sometimes conclude with an account of how the main characters ended up after what is related in the novel. The great (and in places semipornographic)

Chinese novel *The Golden Lotus* ends with an account of what the reincarnations of some of the main characters were.

Buddhist views of human nature are not entirely uniform. We have already seen that some later schools of Buddhism held that human nature is such that we need supernatural help in purifying ourselves; a great many early Buddhists would have denied this. What appears to have been Buddha's view of human nature, however, can be summarized. He believed that initial human nature (before people work on purifying their minds) is given to desires and prone then to suffering. Fulfilled human nature though is rid of any sense of having a substantial self, cleansed of desires, immune to suffering, and compassionate.

Notes

1. See S. Radhakrishnan, ed. and trans., *The Principal Upanishads* (Atlantic Highlands, NJ: Humanities Press, 1992), p. 22.

2. Sydney Shoemaker, "Personal Identity and Memory," in John Perry, ed., *Personal Identity* (Berkeley and Los Angeles: University of California Press, 1975), p. 125.

3. A story by the Argentinean writer Borges, "The Immortal," amusingly exploits this point in the context of an imagined possibility of some people living forever. After a long while they could still remember things that happened, but could not remember whether they happened to them or to someone else—or indeed remember who they are. See Jorge Luis Borges, *Labyrinths*, eds. Donald A. Yates and James Irby (New York: New Directions, 1964), pp. 105–118.

4. This creates complicated questions. As *atman* is defined, your personality is distinct from *atman*. Does this mean that your personality is not identical with Brahman? The answer surely has to be that it is identical. But then it may seem hard to reconcile the idea that the personality is distinct from *atman* with the idea that it is nevertheless identical with Brahman. My thought here goes back to the metaphor of our *atmans* being like drops of water in a spiritual ocean. Personality might be thought of as froth, ice, and steam—the same as water, but in a way not the same.

There is also the question of whether the assertion that all *atmans* are qualitatively the same is compatible with the doctrine of reincarnation. It is often thought that the meaning of a claim or a prediction is tied to how someone might find out whether it is true. Then how can we make sense of a prediction that your *atman* after death will have a more favorable rebirth than will the *atman* of your badly behaved neighbor? It seems unimaginable that anyone would ever find out.

A short answer is that, while knowing whose *atman* is reincarnated in what form might well turn out to be humanly impossible, there is no logical contradiction in imagining that someone might find out. Imaginably a being with supernatural powers (who could, as it were, tag *atmans* the way we tag geese) could track your *atman* from one life to the next. The thought is that there can be a truth of the matter, even if in fact no one knows it.

Questions for Further Consideration

1. The central claim of the *Upanishads* involves an identity between an individual and Brahman (the entire universe). Is this supposed to hold for everyone, or only for most people?

2. Is there anything that you could do (in the view of the *Upanishads*) to enhance your oneness with Brahman?

3. What does Buddha mean by a desire? Is there any reliable way to lose desires?

Recommended Further Reading

Surendranath Dasgupta, *Indian Idealism* (Cambridge: Cambridge University Press, 1962) is a classic account of Indian philosophies, including the ones presented in this chapter. Walpola Rahula, *What the Buddha Taught* (New York: Grove Weidenfeld, 1959) is very readable and reliable.

Chapter 4

Confucius

Confucius (Kongzi), who was roughly contemporary with Buddha, was born (c.550 BCE) in a China in which the empire had disintegrated, only to be replaced by a number of competing kingdoms. Many of the rulers of these kingdoms hoped to conquer some of the other kingdoms, perhaps dreaming of reestablishing a unified empire, though often they had little sense of how to accomplish this.

In the meantime, each ruler exercised absolute power and governed his kingdom (with the aid of officials) in large part for his own benefit. It was extremely dangerous for an official to question the judgment of the ruler. The vast majority of the population consisted of uneducated peasants, who certainly were in no position to question the ruler's demands for taxes or for their work on the ruler's projects.

In this relatively primitive agricultural economy there were stark differences between good years and bad years. In years of bad harvests many people might starve, and if there were two or more bad years in succession, it would be a disaster. Readers who know the Bible might recall the description of a similarly vulnerable population in ancient Egypt, along with Joseph's inspired advice to the pharaoh on how these people could be protected.

All of this is background to what Confucius thought of as his primary mission in life. This chapter will focus chiefly on Confucius' ethics—his account of how life can best be lived—in which his view of human nature is embedded. Confucius said a great deal about human nature and how it can be improved. But his mission was above all to bring good government to China: to replace the selfish and capricious management of the people with a style of government in which their needs were given urgent consideration.

As part of this mission, Confucius traveled from kingdom to kingdom, looking for a ruler who would follow his advice—one who would, in turn, install high officials who would respond conscientiously to the needs of the people. Such a kingdom could serve as a demonstration model of good government and play a major role in winning over the other kingdoms to the ideal. Clearly there was an element of personal ambition in this. Confucius hoped that a ruler could be persuaded to hire him as the high official who would implement the reform program.

From our distant perspective, it may be not surprising that none of this succeeded. At the time though, it must have looked plausible. Some rulers were willing to talk to Confucius. They did not have a clue as to how they could strengthen themselves in relation to their rivals; hence they were willing to listen to anyone who had a new set of ideas. Further, Confucius had a plausible argument. If a kingdom were known to be well governed, in a way that was responsive to the needs of the people, then those who lived in other kingdoms would wish to be governed by that kingdom. In a war, that could make a difference: those in badly governed kingdoms might hope that their side would lose.

Again such a scenario might look hopelessly idealistic. But since the fall of the Berlin Wall, we have been exposed to the possibility that poor government indeed can lead to a loss of power, and good government can lead to an increase of power. Perhaps Confucius' hopes were not entirely unrealistic.

What we are concerned with mainly, in any case, is not Confucius' drive for social reform so much as what he did in the meantime, while he was moving from kingdom to kingdom. He was teaching students, who comprised an extended household that traveled with him. A variety of things were taught, including the early Chinese classics, chiefly the *Book of Odes*.

This collection of poetry (which is available to us as the *Book of Songs* in a translation by Arthur Waley and also one by Ezra Pound) reads like lyrics to folk songs. But Confucius and his students interpreted it as containing coded moral messages. Confucius also taught ritual, which was crucial knowledge for anyone seeking a career as a government official. Above all he had a great deal to say about the management of one's life and about how someone could transform himself (all of the students were male) into a reliably good person.[1]

After Confucius' death, a collection of his sayings—along with some sayings of his principal students—was prepared, and with gradual accretions then over time, this collection became known as the *Analects of Confucius*. It is the source for what we know about Confucius' view of human nature and about the ethics in which it played a part.

The Ethics of Personal Development

A general fact about classic Chinese (and also Indian) philosophy should be kept in mind, especially as a contrast to much of Western ethical philosophy over the last 250 years. The latter has tended to center on a search for decision procedures: general principles or methods that enable you, when you have a moral choice, rationally to arrive at a decision. The ethics of Immanuel Kant, Jeremy Bentham, and John Stuart Mill all exhibit this concern. It also marks John Rawls' study of justice and remains a feature of much recent work in ethical philosophy.

Decision procedures are not entirely neglected in classic Indian and Chinese philosophy, but the main focus is generally on what comprises the optimal development of self for an individual. The usual understanding of the problem is this. We are born with something that might be termed initial human nature. Usually this is not thought of as bad (although one philosopher to be discussed in the next chapter, Xunzi, is sometimes held to tilt in that direction). All the same, initial human nature is by no means ideal. At a certain point in life, we will be capable of modifying and refining this human nature. There are varying prescriptions about the direction in which we should best proceed. The *Upanishads* hold that when we are old enough to understand and take seriously the claim that *atman* is Brahman, we should accustom ourselves increasingly to that way of thinking, in the process giving up thoughts of individuality. Buddha and his early followers hold that when we come to understand and be able to take seriously the link between desire and suffering, we should consider working on ourselves so as to eliminate desires.

Confucius also believed that there is a point—roughly one which his students had reached when they came to him—when someone can realize the possibility of refining original human nature, and in the process becoming a different kind of person. The form that this would take is more difficult to summarize briefly than is the case for the *Upanishads* and for Buddha. In examining it we can get a sense of Confucius' view of fulfilled human nature.

A general formulation of the process is found in *Analects* 1.15.[2] In discussion with Confucius, one of his students repeats a passage from the *Book of Songs:*

As if cut, as if polished;
As if carved, as if ground.

Confucius is delighted at his acuity.

The idea (if this is applied to personal development) is that in early maturity someone can be a sort-of-good person: decent, agreeable, cooperative, and willing to learn. But there can be a transition to becoming a *really* good person. This process will be like cutting away, carving, or grinding some rough and uneven surfaces, and also polishing.

Analects 8.8 sketches the major tools of development from being sort-of-good to the refinement of being a really good person. They are: (1) the classic *Book of Odes* (*Book of Songs*), (2) ritual, and (3) music. Confucius' assumption that the *Book of Songs* contained coded moral messages has already been commented on. Ritual might seem to many in the twenty-first century to be an improbable tool of ethical development. But we should remember that ritual often involves more than one person and requires an appropriate responsiveness to others. It can be thought of as a social dance, which contributes to harmonizing interpersonal interactions. Music, at least of the right sort, plausibly can be regarded as harmonizing emotions. The Greek philosopher Plato held a view of this very much like Confucius'.

What all of this involves can be appreciated against the background of what Confucian ethics is concerned with. Recent Western ethics increasingly has concentrated on moral choices. These are choices that embody some serious matter of principle or in which some significant harm or benefit is at stake, so that a bad choice would be subject to social condemnation and also might well produce feelings of guilt in the offender.

Behavior that merely is foolish or insensitive, as when we hurt the feelings of a friend or inconsiderately make noise when someone is trying to sleep, can be viewed negatively but is not often a philosophical topic.[3] Confucius certainly does talk about some moral choices and takes them seriously. But most of the behavior with which Confucius is concerned is of the more everyday sort, especially in personal relations. A style of thinking and acting that is the result of polishing will be crucial in these.

In the treatment of elderly parents (*Analects* 2.8), for example, "it is the demeanor that is difficult." Confucius certainly subscribed to the traditional view that it was important to see that aged parents got enough to eat, had warm clothes in winter, and so on. But he also realized that if the attitude that accompanied such helpful activities was visibly brusque or grudging, it would ruin the sense of connection.

In short, the reliable goodness that Confucius thought can and should be developed extends to a refined style in everyday interactions as well as to correct moral choices. A telling passage in the *Analects* (1.12) about ritual speaks of the importance of a personal harmony and "harmonious ease." Developing and internalizing such a harmony, Confucius believed, will lead to predictably good moral choices and personal interactions. This will go well beyond being a sort-of-good person.

It may be helpful, in appreciating the force of this idea, to consider the results of some dramatic psychological experiments conducted about fifty years ago. The best known is the Milgram experiment. Milgram's subjects were volunteers who were told that they were participating in an experiment on learning. This in fact was a lie: they actually participated in an experiment on moral corruptibility. The ostensible subject (in fact an actor) sat on the other side of a glass panel from the volunteer, the actual subject. Supposedly the actor was there to answer questions—but in fact gave deliberately wrong answers. The subject's role was to give this person an electric shock, of ever increasing voltage, as the wrong answers multiplied.

In fact there were no real electric shocks, but the actor behaved as if he really had been shocked. As the ostensible voltage of shocks increased, he began to clutch himself in apparent agony and also referred to a heart condition. Many subjects became quite disturbed by this, and wanted to stop their participation. But the man in a white lab coat who was in charge said, in even tones, "The experiment must go on."

It did go on. In the various iterations of the Milgram experiment, first in New Haven and later including college settings (in which the volunteers were students), most subjects went past the point at which the shocks were clearly indicated to be dangerous. A puzzle here is that almost certainly most of these subjects were, in their ordinary lives, reasonably decent, "nice" people. What could account for this apparently hurtful behavior on the part of such individuals?

In recent years some philosophers have suggested that the results of the Milgram experiment (and also of another disturbing study, the Stanford Prison Experiment, in which subjects assigned the roles of guards began to treat their "prisoners" brutally) show that the idea of virtue is faulty. The suggestion is that it is a kind of ethical wishful thinking, attributing stable qualities to individuals. There are good and bad choices, it is argued, but no real virtues—because a person's behavior can vary so much.

We should bear in mind, though, that a number of people (albeit a minority) did refuse to go on with the Milgram experiment. Some walked out at the very beginning, when they understood that they would have to administer electric shocks. Reportedly, one person who walked out when the experiment was performed at Princeton University also was someone who blew the whistle on the infamous My Lai massacre during the Vietnam War.[4]

In short, the Milgram experiment hardly shows that the idea of virtue is an illusion. It arguably shows though that genuine virtue (which will express itself even in difficult or disorienting circumstances) is more rare than most of us would like to think. In addition, it can be argued that virtue is a little more complicated than it might at first appear. If it is true that no one is perfect—but also that some people, on the whole, tend to perform well even in difficult and disorienting circumstances—then an important feature of virtue may be how someone responds to her or his previous lapses. Someone who experiences regret could be able to improve herself or himself to the point of becoming reliable.

All of this is highly relevant to Confucius. Virtue in his view required taking faults and lapses seriously and then working to improve oneself. One student whose lack of moral probity repeatedly disappointed Confucius was Ran Qiu, who appears to have lacked any determination to correct his faults. When Ran Qiu collected taxes to augment the wealth of an already wealthy ruler (*Analects* 11.17)—some of this money presumably coming from poor peasants—Confucius reacted as we would to flagrant immorality and entirely repudiated Ran Qiu.

The need for self-criticism is a repeated theme. Confucius lamented that he had "yet to meet someone who is able to perceive his own faults and then take himself to task inwardly" (*Analects* 5.27). This, however, may have been an exasperated overstatement. The *Analects* quotes Master Zeng as saying that he daily looked for failings in his behavior (1.4). Confucius himself said, "When walking with two other people, I will always find a teacher among them. I focus on those who are good and seek to emulate them, and focus on those who are bad in order to be reminded of what needs to be changed in myself" (7.22). He makes it clear that the process of self-improvement is never finished (7.34).

All of this helps to make it clear that genuine virtue is not equivalent to perfection and that all the same, it is somewhat uncommon—a real achievement in fact. Confucius' implicit map of virtue and badness is shared with some other ancient philosophers, such as Plato and Aristotle. For these philosophers and for Confucius there were a limited number of really virtuous people and perhaps also a limited number of really bad people. The vast majority of people were somewhere in the middle—their behavior depending heavily on circumstances. A nice expression of this is provided by the great Confucian philosopher Mengzi (a.k.a. Mencius, to be discussed in Chapter 6): "In years of plenty, most young men are gentle; in years of poverty, most young men are violent."[5]

Let us return to the Milgram experiment and ask why so many people did things that they later would have been disturbed by. Milgram himself thought that the corrupting influence was deference to authority (that of the psychologist in charge).[6] He referred to a then-current book by Hannah Arendt, *Eichmann in Jerusalem*, which employed the phrase "banality of evil." This was a report of the trial of Adolph Eichmann, a colorless Nazi bureaucrat who had managed the shipment of Jews to death camps. There was no apparent passion in what Eichmann did: he was merely deferring to his Nazi superiors.

In Eichmann's case, though, the Nazi authorities had considerable power, and it might have seemed dangerous not to defer to them. The Milgram experiment was not like this, though something a little like deference to authority may have been a factor in most subjects' compliance. In strange situations, many of us can think that there is a "normal" and right way to proceed, but we have to be told what it is. A psychological experiment might have been in that category for almost all of the subjects, appearing as something that had its own situational etiquette.

Given some time to reflect, perhaps many subjects would have realized that the experiment was going to go beyond any normal limits of behavior. But the experiment was cleverly designed to minimize this likelihood. Everything went fast, and the really awful part (in which you appeared to be giving shocks of high voltage) was reached gradually by stages. Many of us, in most periods of life, mainly tend to carry on rather than make marked shifts in behavior. It takes a special sort of alertness to be able to stop and think, "This is different. I must reflect on this." Not all that many people are good at that.

None of this is an excuse. Indeed, if there were such a thing as a Guide to Corrupting People, it surely would advise creating situations in which a choice had to be made quickly (leaving little time for thought), and would also probably advise moving in gradual stages, arriving at dramatic corruption only by degrees. Real-life corruption often seems to work in this way. If there were a Guide to Not Being Corrupted, it might advise thinking about where all this is leading, and considering where you would draw the line. Being ready, as it were, to "turn on a dime," if there are good reasons, would be part of what is recommended.

Real-life situations in which numbers of people have been corrupted include, most dramatically, those in occupied countries, such as the ones in Europe that the Nazis occupied during World War II. Numbers of people in these countries went along with the new order of things, mainly to avoid trouble. There have been interesting studies of those who did take risks in defying the Nazis. Nechama Tec, in a study of Polish gentiles who at great risk saved Jews from the Nazis, found that a frequent feature of these people was that "they don't blend into their communities."[7]

Confucius mainly focused on the positive—what it would be like to be a genuinely and reliably good person, although he did deal with instances of corruption. He certainly would have agreed with the obvious prescription in Nechama Tec's study, namely, that it is important to be someone who in difficult situations thinks for herself or himself rather than to go along with a kind of group-think. Beyond that, Confucius emphasized the sense of self that one has and would want to maintain.

He also emphasized the importance of being on a path (*dao*) of life. To be thoroughly on a path of goodness is essentially to have no choice in a variety of important matters. This is brought out nicely in a chapter title of Herbert Fingarette's *Confucius:*

The Secular as Sacred– "A Way without a Crossroads."[8] If the idea of not having a choice seems strange to you, ask yourself whether, if someone offered you a lot of money to torture a baby, you would have a choice.

Initial Human Nature and
Ideal Second Nature

Initial human nature in Confucius' view definitely included powerful influences of unreasonable appetites. Thus he remarks in the *Analects*, "I have yet to meet a man who loves Virtue as much as he loves female beauty" (9.18). There are similar remarks about desires for wealth (4.5 and 8.12).

We should not assume, I think, that these observations mean that someone of developed character might not appreciate an attractive partner or some additional money. They do imply, however, that beauty and wealth should count as lesser values than the possession of virtue and that these lesser values should not be pursued in any way that compromises virtue. If this is correct, then Confucius' view is similar to that of Aristotle, who regards "external" goods as counting toward a person's *eudaemonia* (well-being) but as less important than the exercise of virtues is.

Ideal second nature for Confucius would not only include virtue but also would include the enjoyment of virtue. This point is made concisely in *Analects* 4.2: "Without Goodness, one cannot remain constant in adversity and cannot enjoy enduring happiness." As so often in the *Analects*, the reader is given the gist of an idea and is left to think about its ramifications and also to figure out why it would be correct. We will pursue these explanations in what follows.

The Rewards of Fulfilled Human Nature

We can begin by reflecting on what might be required to be constant in adversity. Outward behavior could remain constant if one had a firm policy and adhered to it. All the same, the temptation not to be firm could become strong. "Why bother, when things are going so badly?" might be an obvious thought. Constancy in one's thoughts might be an even more difficult matter. Think of Job in the Bible. When almost all the people and things he cared about had been taken away from him, he avoided unworthy thoughts; but there definitely was a change in mood, and a lot of depressed thoughts.

How can someone endure adversity without a drastic mind shift? One obvious answer is that it is possible if one retains major positive values. Many philosophers have drawn a contrast between "external" values, such as money, reputation, power, and so on, and "internal" values. The latter concern what you are like, as it were, "inside" and what your relationship is to yourself.

Analects 6.20 extols the kind of person who takes joy in the Confucian way. This may seem strange, an example of what might be called philosophical boosterism. It looks much less strange if one takes into account empirical findings in the psychology of happiness. Michael Argyle reports findings that give self-esteem a major role in personal happiness. The aspects of personality that he says are associated quite strongly with happiness include internal control, absence of inner conflicts, and involvement with goal-directed work and leisure.[9]

To appreciate this, we have to rid ourselves of the superficial idea that pleasure and happiness are virtually equivalent, or at least very closely related, emotional experiences. There are many important differences. One is in typical duration: pleasures tend to be brief, whereas happiness can last for months or years at a time. Also, pleasures have objects: one takes pleasure in a thing or an experience. It is possible to be happy about nothing in particular—perhaps about life or the world.

One difference that is definitely relevant to Confucius' view is that it is possible for someone not to like herself or himself, and yet to experience pleasures. Argyle's data strongly suggest that such a person would not be happy. This is because the sense of self matters so much in happiness.

With this in mind, let us consider the happiness of someone who has achieved the fulfilled state of a really virtuous second nature. In adversity such a person could lose various external goods, but major sources (really, *the* major sources) of satisfaction would remain. Being able to maintain a positive view of oneself counts for a lot. Beyond this, we should remember that Confucian goodness is exercised not only in large moral choices but also in dozens of daily personal interactions. There will be a lot of benign skill at work in these.

The psychologist Milhaly Csikszentmihalyi has found that people consider their most satisfying experiences to be ones in which they are absorbed in skilled activities, which as it were flow along.[10] Someone with (by Confucian standards) an entirely fulfilled second nature would be, in a way, constantly engaged in skilled performances: being good with people in personal interactions and displaying a harmonious ease in ritual. Even if money and prestige had drained away, this would represent a reservoir of satisfaction conducive to being constant in adversity.

Such a person also would enjoy enduring happiness. "Surely happiness is to be enjoyed and then would continue to be enjoyed?" a reader might think. Recall that *Analects* 4.2, which speaks to this, claims that while someone who does not have a fulfilled second nature certainly can enjoy periods of happiness, the happiness would not endure. Only a thoroughly good person would be able not only to experience happiness but also to have it last.

One of the reasons why this is true is given in *Analects* 7.37. It involves the ongoing attitude toward what awaits one in life. Confucius says, "The gentleman (i.e., someone of refined virtue) is self-possessed and relaxed, while the petty man is perpetually full of worry." The reason for this is straightforward. If what matters most to you in life are the internal values related to sense of self, then you realize that these are very largely within your control. This will help you to be self-possessed and relaxed, because you are not really very vulnerable.

You do have some control over external values such as money and prestige, but much less. These values are very vulnerable to bad luck. So the "petty man," who cares mainly about such external values, has a lot to worry about.

A second reason is the psychological force that the Greeks called *pleonexia*. This is the tendency, for people invested in certain areas of life perpetually to want more of whatever they already have got. This tendency is especially conspicuous in relation to wealth. People who have considerable amounts of money—more than it would normally be thought anyone really needs—very often find themselves wanting more. Perhaps a competitive sense—in relation to other wealthy people—plays a part in this? Someone to whom reputation and prestige really matter (and this can include writers, artists, and philosophers) may similarly, having experienced some success, very much want even more.

The force of *pleonexia* can be intermittent. Someone who has just acquired a considerable amount of money or who has won a prize and had some very good reviews may simply be happy. It may take a little while before *pleonexia* kicks in and the desire for more (or for higher status) grows. When *pleonexia* is a factor, happiness does not endure in any steady, uninterrupted way. If, on the other hand, we assume that fulfilled human nature will have eliminated *pleonexia,* then (given satisfaction with internal values), someone who has appropriately refined her or his nature can experience enduring happiness.

Genuine Personal Goodness and Good Government

Let us return briefly, in conclusion, to Confucius' primary concern with good government. His core belief was that there would be good government if and only if those who ran the government (which included high officials as well as the ruler) were, at least for the most part, genuinely good people. Some of the reasons for this were obvious. Those who were genuinely good would have more concern for the well-being of the people, including the peasants, than had been typical in the Chinese kingdoms. This concern would result in effective choices. To be concerned about others is to be more likely to think about what they need and how best they can be helped.

Beyond this, there is the factor of role modeling, as noted in *Analects* 2.1. One feature of role modeling is that those high up set an emotional tone. Constancy or stability is crucial to goodness (13.22). The official or ruler of refined goodness, who has got beyond *pleonexia*, can set a tone of calmness and consideration for others, which can do a great deal to promote a good society. Such a society will, in turn, be more conducive to the achievement of fulfilled human nature on the part of its members.

Notes

1. To a modern reader the invisibility of women in Confucius' *Analects* can be disturbing. It could be argued that Confucius and his close associates were simply, as it were, carrying the baggage of the culture at that time. A complicating factor in thinking about the possible roles of women in a philosophy like Confucius' is that the one school of current ethical philosophy that has strong similarities (in what it focuses on) to Confucius' philosophy is feminist ethics. For a variety of views on this complicated subject, see *The Sage and the Second Sex*, ed. Chenyang Li (Chicago: Open Court, 2000).

2. Confucius, *Analects*, trans. Slingerland pp. 6–7.

3. There are some exceptions to this pattern of largely ignoring normative nonmoral judgments (including those involved in personal relations). The largest exception is feminist ethics. One way of viewing the split between moral judgments and nonmoral normative judgments is offered by John Stuart Mill. In paragraph 14 of Chapter 5 of *Utilitarianism*, Mill observes that we do not call something morally wrong "unless we mean to imply that a person ought to be punished in some way or other for doing it—if not by law, by the opinion of his fellow creatures; if not by opinion, by the reproaches of his own conscience." Chapter 4 of Mill's *On Liberty* would appear to indicate that while we normally respond

with hostility to violation of a "distinct and assignable obligation," an appropriate response to foolish or tasteless behavior (or, I think, generally insensitive behavior in personal relations) is to avoid such a person, perhaps also admonishing him. See *On Liberty*, ed. Elizabeth Rapaport (Indianapolis: Hackett Publishing Co., 1978), pp. 75 and 77. The phrase "distinct and assignable obligation" is on p. 79.

4. Personal communication from the cultural anthropologist Richard Schweder, April 5, 1996, reconfirmed February 23, 2000.

5. *Mengzi*, trans. Bryan W. Van Norden (Indianapolis: Hackett Publishing Co., 2008), 4.A.7, p. 150.

6. Cf. Stanley Milgram, *Obedience to Authority* (London: Tavistock, 1974).

7. Nechama Tec, *When Light Pierced the Darkness: Christians' Rescue of Jews in Nazi-Occupied Poland* (New York: Oxford University Press, 1986), pp. 188–189.

8. *Confucius: The Secular As Sacred* (Long Grove, IL: Waveland Press, 1998), Chapter 2.

9. Michael Argyle, *The Psychology of Happiness* (London: Methuen and Co., 1987), p. 124.

10. Mihaly Csikszentmihalyi, *Flow: The Psychology of Optimal Experience* (New York: Harper and Row, 1990).

Questions for Further Consideration

1. Transforming yourself into a different (and better) kind of person is not an easy job. Does Confucius' view imply that anyone can accomplish this?

2. Is there any truth to the idea that the major requirement for good government is to have highly virtuous people making the decisions?

Recommended Further Reading

Herbert Fingarette, *Confucius: The Secular as Sacred* (Long Grove, IL: Waveland Press, 1998) is a well regarded analytic account of Confucius' philosophy. Philip J. Ivanhoe, *Confucian Moral Self-Cultivation* (Indianapolis: Hackett Publishing Co., 2000) is an exceptionally clear and readable account of Confucianism.

Chapter 5

Plato and Aristotle
(and Some Freudian Echoes of Plato):
Parts of the Mind That Can
Achieve a Proper Harmony

Plato and Aristotle each had a view of human nature that assigned reason a central role. This to a large extent reflected the ancient Greek preoccupation (noted in Chapter 1) with the difference between humans and animals. Whatever relatively unimportant similarities to animals we might have, the important thing is that we human beings are—or at least could be—rational. Aristotle's view was that man (i.e., the human being) is the rational animal, period. Plato's view had been more complex. This reflected his interest in deficient human beings (such as tyrants) who in many respects are irrational, and also his very high standard of rationality. His sense was that people *could be* highly rational animals and that some of us are.

Plato came first, living in Athens during the fifth and fourth centuries BCE. Like Confucius, who about a century earlier had suggested a parallel between personal goodness and good government, Plato thought that a good division among the parts of a human soul paralleled a good division among the classes of people within a commonwealth. The best part of the soul, in Plato's view, was reason; and the best group within a commonwealth consisted of the most rational people. Reason,

Plato thought, should govern within the soul, and the most rational people should govern within a commonwealth.

Besides reason, the soul in Plato's account included a spirited element—which was fine as long as it was governed by reason—and also an appetitive element, which also was fine as long as our appetites were constrained so that they were within reason. The spirited element corresponded roughly to the warrior class in a society, and the appetitive element corresponded to the farmers and producers and more broadly to the ordinary people who would be consumers. Both in a society and in an individual soul, these divisions were very acceptable as long as reason was in charge.

The notion that reason should be in charge, both personally and politically, has immediate plausibility. The harmony of elements that this is said to promote also has a strong appeal. Most of us do not relish inner conflicts or for that matter class warfare within a society. Further, it could be argued that the opposite of the personality that Plato recommends is the neurotic individual, who is at cross-purposes with himself or herself. This kind of inner conflict diminishes effectiveness and can lead to grief.

We can begin our investigation by looking more closely at Plato's view and then looking at Aristotle's account and also at Freud's Plato-like mapping of a divided soul. In any philosophical investigation, the hardest questions may concern the meanings of seemingly simple key terms. In particular, it is easy to talk about "reason." But do we know what we are talking about?

Plato's View of Reason

Plato followed the view of Socrates, his teacher, that to have knowledge one must be able to define one's terms. It seems curious then that he has given us no clear definition of what reason is. An unsympathetic reader might wonder whether *reason* can be defined. Someone who has been immersed in twentieth-century philosophy indeed might wonder whether many of the terms that are widely used in philosophy are capable of being defined.

Most people tend to think that terms in common use can be given entirely adequate definitions, and this is part of our faith in dictionaries. But perhaps the definitions, helpful though they may be, are rarely or never entirely adequate? The case for thinking this was put forth by Ludwig Wittgenstein in his *Philosophical Investigations* (1953). Wittgenstein's view was that, while terms created for some special discipline (e.g., *volt* or *watt*) could be given entirely adequate definitions, this generally was not possible for words in ordinary language. His example was the word *game*. We all know what a game is. But can we specify a set of necessary and sufficient conditions so that something counts as a game if and only if it meets these conditions?[1]

Wittgenstein's answer was no. One might think of a game as a competition in which there is winning and losing. But wars meet this standard, and we do not normally think of wars as games. The obvious next thought is that we need to insist on playfulness: a game then could be defined as a playful competition in which there is winning or losing. But professional football games are not exactly playful. Putting that to the side, we might think of ring-around-the-rosy, a child's game in which there is no winning or losing.

What Wittgenstein suggests is that our idea of a game will center on some obvious examples (e.g., football, chess, poker), which nowadays would be spoken of as "paradigm cases." We then regard activities that are similar to these central examples as also counting as games. The similarity can be in various respects. Wittgenstein's phrase is "family resemblances." Games resemble other games much as a member of the Jones family might resemble other members by having the typical Jones nose or might not have the typical Jones nose but have the body build and mannerisms often found in the Jones family.

Much of Wittgenstein's point had been anticipated in the nineteenth century in John Stuart Mill's *System of Logic*. "General names," Mill said, ". . . connote little more than a vague gross resemblance to the things which they were earliest, or have been most, accustomed to call by those names." In short, "a name is not imposed at once and by previous purpose on a *class* of objects, but is first applied to one thing, and then extended by a series of transitions to another and another."[2]

What Mill and Wittgenstein said suggests that perhaps reason simply cannot be defined in any entirely adequate way. The best we can do is to point out some clear examples of reason. Here are two: mathematical thought and logical inferences. Logical inferences can be subdivided into deductive interferences (which explore how, given certain premises, a conclusion must be true) and inductive inferences (which explore how, given a certain pattern in the real world, it is likely that something that fits that pattern will happen). Reason (in deductive thought) can tell us what assuredly is implicit in our assumptions or premises. It also (in inductive thought) sometimes can tell us what is likely in an unfamiliar case or in the future, basing this on what has been true in the past.

These are clear examples. However, any reader of Plato knows that, in his view, knowing what the proper idea of "good" is and knowing which kinds of things are good also represents the working of reason. Indeed there is a famous story of Plato's announcing that he would give a lecture on the good, and its then turning out that the lecture (which unfortunately has not been preserved) was about mathematics.

Sadly, value theory (along with other parts of ethics) is not mathematics. Is it much like mathematics or logic? There is this resemblance. Mathematical and logical thinking represent highly developed, and generally precise, kinds of intelligence at work. Awareness of value, and more broadly being able to arrive at sound judgments of value also represent intelligence at work. The intelligence in the case of goodness may well be more intuitive and personal than mathematics or logic is. It also is debatable whether it can be at all precise.

The Mill-Wittgenstein account can help us to understand not only Plato's assimilation of knowledge of the good to reason but also a good deal in our normal way of talking about how people successfully perform in thought and in life. Here are a few examples of outlying uses of the concepts of "reason" or "being rational." If a bright student is about to drop out of college in order to experience riding around the country in freight trains, friends might attempt to get him or her to "listen to reason." If someone in a difficult situation "loses it" and becomes wildly emotional, the advice might be "Try to be rational." If you become aware of a feature that you think helps to make an experience highly desirable (or the reverse), or a feature that makes a work of art beautiful (or worthless), you may point to that feature as a "reason" for your evaluation of the experience or the work of art.

Those who urge the bright student not to drop out of college could simply say, "Don't be stupid". This, however, sounds harsh and might be counterproductive. It is more effective to remind the potential dropout of his or her capacity to think intelligently. Saying "listen to reason" is a convenient way of accomplishing this.

Similarly, the wildly emotional person could simply be reminded that we all tend to think more clearly when we are not in the grip of strong emotions. "Be rational" is a succinct way of saying this. It draws on traditional contrasts between emotions and reason.

These contrasts are now widely thought by philosophers and psychologists to be oversimplistic. Some mild emotions (such as compassion for someone who is suffering or delight in something lovely) are justified by features in their objects. Almost everyone would agree that they are eminently "reasonable," which means that such emotions can count as appropriate and really right on the part of the people who have them.

We often do have reasons for valuing (or disvaluing) experiences or works of art. Often to give a "reason" is to call attention to the value-promoting feature. Is there a logical relation of some sort between the existence of the feature and a value judgment that it supports? This question is hard to answer.

Some years ago I argued that the answer was a qualified yes.[3] But there might be grounds for a more hesitant answer. One is that a feature can be value-promoting in one context and not in others, and some logicians would insist on fixed relations between a logical starting point and a logical conclusion.

It also should be said that even if there is some kind of weak logical relation (definitely weaker than entailment) between description and evaluation, this hardly means that the value judgment typically results from a rational process or a process of reasoning.

However one judges this, we could as easily speak of a "basis" or a "ground" for an evaluation as speak of "a reason." If we do speak of a reason, which seems harmless enough given how we normally talk, this should not lead us to assume that there is some close connection between having a reason and the core activities of reasoning. Much more often than not, such activities do not occur when we arrive at evaluative judgments.

Cases of the sorts described involve appeals to intelligence. Words like *reason* and *rational* gesture at this feature. The gesturing is harmless, unless one is led to make the mistake of supposing that what has a reason or is rational must involve a process of reasoning. These cases are not much like what goes on in mathematics or logic.

Some words are like the sticky paper that traps flies and mice. The word *reason* sometimes traps philosophers, especially nowadays. It may be that a desire to protect the territory of philosophy plays a part in this. So many areas of what used to be considered philosophy have been lost to empirical disciplines, such as the natural sciences, psychology, and linguistics.

It can seem important to retain philosophy's claim to everything that involves reason and logic. This thought, however, can lead to an especially expansive use of the word *reason* to characterize varieties of intelligent thought that really have very little to do with logic or mathematics and do not have much similarity to them. This introduces a rhetorical feature into a subject that is not supposed to have such features.

All the same, it may well be that there are kinds of ordinary intelligent thinking that philosophy can appropriately examine and also promote. Need this philosophical attention be excused on the grounds that these are really varieties of reason? It is hard to think that excuse is needed.

Where Plato Stands

To return to Plato: his reasons for assimilating intelligent thought about values to reason surely were different from what motivates philosophers today. We can appreciate Plato best if we explore his attitudes toward sameness and change. These are reflected in his conception of what constitutes knowledge.

The crucial distinction for Plato was between what changes and what remains the same, or between "becoming" and "being." It is hard for a philosopher to deny that things in the world in some sense change. One of Plato's predecessors, Heraclitus, was very alive to this. His most famous saying (previously mentioned) was that you could not step in the same river twice. The point is that even in rather little time there will be minor changes. Of course we continue to give the slightly changed river the same name: this is enormously convenient, much more sensible than trying to assign a new name every few minutes. But the name represents an artificial, constructed identity. Really, the river is not the same.

We in the twenty-first century, in considering this, might not see any difficulty in holding that we can have knowledge of things or objects that change. Also in classical Chinese philosophy, especially in Daoism (which emphasized a degree of harmony with the world and lack of confrontation with its developments), that was considered to be a central truth about knowledge of the world. It implied that we had to be flexible and open in our approach if we were to function at all intelligently.

Plato would have none of this. In his view, there were paradigmatic examples of real knowledge, and these set the standard for what knowledge is. Any ability to understand changing events and to say correct things (including predictions of what would happen) about them could have some minor value. But by the standard of mathematics or of our knowledge of essences (which Plato referred to as forms), this would not come up to the level of real knowledge. It would rather be some form of opinion—intelligent opinion perhaps—but still opinion rather than knowledge.

Alfred North Whitehead and others have suggested that Plato has had a lasting influence on Western thought. It would be wrong to suggest that all successful Western philosophers or scientists are in some sense Platonists. There have been, and are, enormous variations in approaches to knowledge (or putative knowledge) of change. All the same, one might discern some differences between Western thought since Plato and Chinese thought since the Daoists and Confucius. The latter often has paid considerable attention to multiplicity of detail and to context. The former has tended to pay considerable attention to abstractions and unchanging truths. Western attention to objects also tends to dwell on conspicuous central features. The psychologist Richard Nisbett recently has studied part of this contrast in an interesting book.[4]

It is abundantly obvious that Plato considered our mastery of mathematical and logical truths to be prime examples of knowledge of being. Are there other examples of knowledge? Knowledge of the good comes to mind.

Plato said that in the highest kind of knowledge (which is knowledge of the good), the knower becomes the known. In other words, knowledge of the good is personally transformative. If someone says the right things about what is good but does not seem strongly committed in that direction, it would count as opinion and not as knowledge.[5] For example, if a man says that it is very important to help the poor but does nothing when given the opportunity, we would be inclined to doubt that he *knows* that helping the poor is important.

The possibility also seems to be left open that knowledge of the good could have an intuitive character. Does all of this mean that it is not knowledge of "being"? Not necessarily. It is possible to hold that a suitably prepared faculty of reason will immediately gravitate to timeless truths about the good.

Freud's Three Parts of the Human Personality

Some readers will recognize immediately a reference to the superego, the ego, and the id. The superego represents the norms of conscience, and more broadly our better judgments of what acceptable behavior should be like. The id, conversely, represents cravings and desires that we might barely admit to ourselves. The ego is our reflective sense of what is intelligent and appropriate behavior that would make sense for us.

Do these correspond closely to Plato's threefold portrayal (in *The Republic*) of reason, the spirited element, and the appetitive dimension? In one detail the parallel is not extremely close. In Freud's picture, the middle element (the ego) has the primary role in deciding. Plato clearly held that reason (which might seem to correspond more to the superego than to the ego) should be in control. However, in Plato's *Phaedrus*, there is a different portrayal of the human self that seems much closer to Freud's. The image is of a charioteer and two horses. One horse corresponds to our better self (much like the superego) and the other to our less well-governed self (reminiscent of the id). The charioteer controls these, and steers them (and us) through life. This will seem very like the ego.

One feature of the story in the *Phaedrus* of the charioteer and the two horses deserves special comment. Someone who sees life, as Hollywood films often do, as a war between extreme goodness and extreme evil might think, "Why doesn't the charioteer simply kill (instead of merely controlling) the bad horse?" It is clear what Plato's answer to this would be. The bad horse may represent the lower side of ourself; but all the same it is useful, and plays a significant role in life.

The reasons for this are not fully spelled out. However, some modern philosophers have thought that our "lower desires"— including ones that should not be acted on (and that might remind some people of products of the id)—are sources of energy. To eliminate them or nearly eliminate them is to risk having a much-reduced level of energy. The trick is not straightforwardly to act them out but rather to sublimate in productive ways the momentum that they represent.[6] This channels the energy, and we can do this without doing anything that we would be ashamed of.

To return to Freud: besides his division among the three main functioning psychological elements (superego, ego, and id), there is another division worth noting. This is between the conscious mind and the unconscious. Included in the unconscious are thoughts or experiences that have been repressed, either as too painful or as unacceptable. Wishes we cannot avow to ourselves, for example, can remain in the unconscious. They then can appear, in disguised form, in dreams, or emerge in accidents or in slips of the tongue.

The dutiful function of the mind (the superego) in short can remain powerful (in some cases, perhaps too powerful?) in the conscious portion of the mind. But down below, as it were, and in dreams and stumbles, there can be many hidden little acts of rebellion.

Aristotle: Man as the Rational Animal

Aristotle was a biologist as well as a philosopher. He also had a more complicated view of causation than the one that has been common in the West in the last few centuries. He distinguished four separate senses in which something can be said to be the cause of something else.

The two that concern us are the efficient cause and the final cause. The efficient cause corresponds to what nowadays we would speak of as "the cause." It is what makes something happen or be the case. The final cause is the end or purpose that leads to something's happening or being the case. (Of the remaining two causes, the formal cause is the nature of the thing; the material cause is what it is made of.)

Armed with the four causes, we can ask how we would distinguish humans from other animals. Humanity has many special features. One might conceivably define man as the joke-telling animal, or the crossword-solving animal, or the animal that often reminisces. All of these, however, can be accounted for in terms of broader capacities, such as mastery of language, an articulate sense of time, and the ability to contrast regularities with what is incongruous.

In some extremely broad sense of rational and reason, all of this could be put under the heading of being rational or possessing reason. Further, a biologist can recognize that the effective flourishing of an organism is a final cause of its being rational. That is, the effective flourishing of the organism is the goal in relation to which we can understand the function of rationality.

When biologists analyze a kind of organism, they tend to focus most on cases in which things function as they should. Arms, legs, hearts, and lungs in some cases do not function properly, and this too will be described. But the starting point usually is what a kind of organism is like when it is functioning effectively.

Aristotle was aware that people sometimes are irrational. Indeed there are a few extreme cases of people who are rarely or never rational. But in differentiating humans from other organisms, he, of course, concentrated on what normally obtains and makes possible effective functioning of a human organism.

Hence it is important that man is the rational animal. What this is the final cause of says a great deal about what is to count as human flourishing. In the *Nicomachean Ethics,* Aristotle rejected the view that a life devoted to pleasures or in which honor and prestige are central will amount to *eudaemonia,* which is his term for a highly desirable state of well-being. Aristotle insisted that the best kind of human life will feature not merely the possession but also the activation of the virtues. Some virtues are moral or civic. But the most highly regarded ones, he thought, should be the "intellectual" virtues, which require excellence in contemplative areas, such as philosophy and mathematics. What might be grouped under the heading of human "rationality" has as its final cause the desirability of a life suffused with such virtues.

Notes

1. See *Philosophical Investigations,* trans. G. E. M. Anscombe (London: Macmillan & Co., 1953), p. 31e, No. 66 ff.

2. John Stuart Mill, *System of Logic* (London: Longmans, Green, and Co., 1884), Book I, Chapter VIII, 7, pp. 98–99; italics Mill's.

3. Cf. "A New Look at the Logic of the 'Is'-'Ought' Relation," *Philosophy* 80, no. 313 (July 2005): 343–359.

4. See Richard Nisbett, *The Geography of Thought: How Culture Colors the Way the Mind Works* (New York: Free Press, 2003).

5. This point is taken up by the nineteenth-century philosopher Søren Kierkegaard. He draws a contrast between ethical and ethico-religious knowledge, on one hand, and other forms of knowledge (including scientific knowledge) on the other. See *Concluding Unscientific Postscript,* trans. David F. Swenson and Walter Lowrie (Princeton: Princeton University Press, 1941), pp. 176–177. You could have the latter kind of knowledge without any effect on the kind of person you are. This is not true of ethical or ethico-religious knowledge.

6. Something like this thought can be found in the nineteenth-century philosopher Friedrich Nietzsche's *Thus Spake Zarathustra,* in which "going under" (sublimation) is a recurrent theme.

Questions for Further Consideration

1. When Plato talks about the rational part of the soul and how it should dominate, what is he recommending to each of us about our lives?

2. If Plato is right, why not just try to eliminate the other parts of our souls?

3. When Aristotle maintains that man is the rational animal, what does this amount to? Does it imply that every student ought to be able to do 'A' work?

Recommended Further Reading

A broad overview of the philosophical context is provided by Frederick Copleston, *A History of Philosophy,* vol. 1, *Greece and Rome* (London: Burns Oates & Washbourne, 1956). R. M. Hare's *Plato* (Oxford: Oxford University Press, 1982) is readable and useful. *Aristotle's Ethics,* edited by Nancy Sherman (Lanham, MD: Rowman and Littlefield, 1999) provides a good sense of varying views on Aristotle.

Chapter 6

Mengzi and Xunzi: The Capacity for True Benevolence

Mengzi (widely known in the West as Mencius) and Xunzi (Hsun-Tzu) are generally classified as Confucians, carrying forward some aspects of Confucius' philosophy.[1] Mengzi flourished in the fourth century BCE and Xunzi in the third century. They both believed in Confucius' ideal of a refined person who was both benevolent and public spirited. They both (like Confucius) regarded such a role as one that no one is born into. Rather it will be the product of good education and work on oneself.

Despite this convergence of views, Mengzi and Xunzi are frequently portrayed as opposites. The simple picture is that Mengzi believed that human nature is good and Xunzi believed that it is evil. That this is a gross oversimplification will soon become apparent. But all the same, there is a sharp difference between the best-known views of the two with regard to initial human nature: that is, the nature with which we are born and that we display in varying ways when we are children.

About two thousand years after Mengzi, the English philosopher John Locke portrayed the mind at birth as a blank tablet (in Latin, *tabula rasa*). Locke's empiricist philosophy held that knowledge mainly comes from sense experience that writes on the mind, contributing finally to a mind that has many ideas and tendencies. Very few philosophers or psychologists nowadays would portray the mind at birth as a blank tablet. It is generally accepted that each of us is born with a temperament, which involves individual tendencies to behave and respond in certain ways. Further, there are widely shared kinds of infant behavior, including ways of responding to signs of distress from other infants. These will be discussed shortly.

Mengzi and Benevolence

Mengzi's most distinctive claim was that initial human nature includes a tendency sometimes to feel benevolent toward others, especially others who clearly are in distress or are suffering. It is important to bear in mind the cautiousness of this claim, controversial though it is. Mengzi does not assert that initial human nature includes a tendency to be generally and consistently benevolent. He is well aware that we all have various selfish motivations and that these often have more influence on us than any benevolent disposition is likely to have. Further, the initial tendency toward benevolence is (to adapt a horticultural metaphor) more like a sprout or a seed than like any developed sturdy plant.

It is important to emphasize these qualifications in Mengzi's claim that there is an element of benevolence in initial human nature. A casual summary of his claim might be that human nature is good. But that would be misleading. At most, what he said is that there is something good in human nature. Given the thought that there is a lot in initial human nature that is far less lovely, we can see that this is a very modest claim.

A recent line of thought that connects with Mengzi highlights both the limited nature of Mengzi's central claim and also its plausibility. The great eighteenth-century Scottish philosopher David Hume (to be discussed in Chapter 9) held a view of human nature that is remarkably similar to Mengzi's, even though he probably had never heard of Mengzi. Hume also maintained that there is an element of benevolence in normal human nature, while recognizing that there are strong tendencies toward various forms of selfish behavior as well.

What makes this convergence especially striking is that their similar views grow out of sharply different preoccupations and projects. Mengzi is first and foremost concerned with the traditional Confucian project of getting some people not merely to be sort-of-good people but to develop into deeply (and reliably) good people. His claim that there is an element of benevolence in normal human nature is intended to show that each of us has, as it were, the psychological wherewithal to launch us in the project of refining ourselves so as to be thoroughly good.

Hume, as we will see later, is not involved in that project. His preoccupation had a lot to do with the views of one of his predecessors, Thomas Hobbes. Hobbes had portrayed human nature as basically self-interested. Hume was concerned to show that there was more to the story than that. He also had a puzzle to solve: that of making sense of the development of a widely shared morality (to which everyone intelligibly could appeal) among people who are largely self-interested. The solution to this puzzle, Hume contended, lay in the shared element of benevolence, on which could be built a common point of view in certain matters.

To return to Mengzi: he believed that there are imaginable situations in which almost anyone would rise to the occasion in a benevolent way.[2] His carefully chosen example involves a situation in which a child is about to fall into a well (thereby presumably to drown). Almost anyone, he contends, would sympathize with the child in danger, hoping that it would not drown.

The element of benevolence might emerge even in relation to an animal. Very early in the *Mengzi* we are given the story of a king who spared the life of an ox that was about to be sacrificed. When Mengzi asks him about the incident, he acknowledges that he was touched by the fear in the animal's eyes. The story though depicts what amounts to moral ambivalence. The sacrifice had to take place. So the king ordered the sacrifice of a sheep, which he did not see.

In short, the king—like almost all of us—was benevolent but also (especially from the sheep's point of view) not benevolent. Further, it is no accident that he was benevolent when he could see the fear in a prospective victim's eyes, as opposed to being not benevolent when he could not see the victim. Relative indifference to what one cannot see can be a serious matter. As Mengzi points out to the king, large numbers of the people over whom he rules are in a precarious condition (partly because of his policies) and are highly vulnerable to suffering. But the king does not see them and allows the conditions that threaten them to continue.

Once we take all this in, we can see that there are two possible levels of benevolence. One involves stray benevolent impulses, generally brought on by visible distress or at least by some need that we can see. The impulse to hope the child does not fall into the well and drown is of this sort. Even a fairly nasty person— say, a criminal—might well have a benevolent impulse in such a situation.

A much higher level of benevolence is systematic rather than occasional and extends to people and animals that we do not see.[3] This higher level requires considerable thoughtfulness. A king can have a major effect on the lives of poor peasants, depending on his tax policy and depending also on whether he carefully stores surpluses from years of good harvests so that people will not starve when there are years of bad harvests. Mengzi, who like Confucius (Kongzi) believed strongly in social responsibility (and like him could be termed a "do-gooder"), traveled around China as Kongzi had, in an unsuccessful attempt to find a king who would be systematically benevolent toward his people.

A major problem is, as the proverb has it, "out of sight, out of mind." There is a better chance (although hardly one with extremely high probability) that someone will behave well toward people that she or he can see than toward those who are unseen. A dramatic suggestion during the late-twentieth-century cold war between the Soviet Union and America was based on this. For some decades each country had nuclear missiles aimed at the other, which could be fired by the push of a button. Once launched, they would kill millions. The ruler of the Soviet Union and the president of the United States each had a button.

At one point, someone suggested an agreement between the two countries, which would require some American children to be hostages in Russia and some Russian children to be hostages in America. The agreement would be that neither the Soviet premier nor the American president would fire the nuclear missiles without first personally killing the child hostages. Let me hasten to say that this was surely not a serious suggestion. Rather, it was intended to dramatize the point that it would be psychologically easier to press a button to kill millions of unseen people than it would be to kill (up close and personally) a few children. Mengzi would have immediately recognized the point.

There is one other respect in which Mengzi's claim that human beings have an element of benevolence turns out to be qualified. There can be exceptions: that is, people who never have a benevolent impulse. Mengzi used a horticultural analogy for this, imagining a mountain that initially is covered with vegetation. But repeated episodes of animals grazing and consuming the vegetation can lead to the mountain becoming bald. This points toward a complicated account of the prevalence of an element of benevolence. On one hand, the suggestion is that initial human nature will contain such an element. But the suggestion also is that repeated circumstances of life that are unfavorable to benevolence can cause someone to lose any element of benevolence. Here again, there is a parallel in Hume's philosophical psychology. Hume offered the wicked Emperor Nero as an example of someone who lost his humanity, and mentions the ancient Scythians, who took scalps, also as inhuman.

Thus far the discussion of Mengzi's view of benevolence has been concerned largely with bringing out how guarded Mengzi's claim is. A separate question is whether Mengzi's limited claim was right. Does normal human nature—especially initial human nature—include an element of benevolence?

Some research by the psychologist Martin L. Hoffman points toward an answer of yes. He found in very young children patterns of empathetic distress responding to and sharing the distress of other very young children.[4] This is perhaps not entirely the same as benevolence but would seem to point in that direction.

To sum up: Mengzi provided a highly plausible case for sprouts of benevolence being part of normal human nature. This does not mean that we are all good human beings. It does, however, indicate that we have something to work with as we try to transform ourselves from sort-of-good people to deeply good people. Xunzi also was concerned with this sort of transformation. However, he had a different view of the starting points and a somewhat different view as well of the process.

Xunzi on Human Improvement

In Xunzi's view, initial human nature is crude and unreliable. Compared to the nature of a civilized and refined human being, initial human nature is like warped wood. It needs to be straightened out.

This view arguably is not as hostile as a bald summary of it might seem. First of all, it is compatible with the idea that these warped, uncivilized humans have positive potential. If we hold that idea, we can think of small children as sometimes charming barbarians, of whom something could be made. (But then, what do they know?)

Are they evil? The moral unreliability of, say, two-year-olds would be an interesting topic in its own right. Moral unreliability, however, is not tantamount to what we normally consider evil. Many adults of normal intelligence are morally unreliable but would not be considered evil (merely thoughtless and impulsively selfish). The word *evil* usually implies a recurrent preference for harm to others over what is good for others. But much adult bad behavior does not involve such a preference; rather it is the expression of a determined selfishness along with thoughtlessness and insensitivity about likely effects on others.

In short, to summarize Xunzi's view as being that initial human nature is evil is a dramatic overstatement. His position is not as sharply different from that of Mengzi as simplistic summaries can make it sound. Indeed, it looks possible for someone to accept Mengzi's claim that there is a sprout of benevolence in normal human nature and, at the same time, to accept much of what Xunzi says. Much of the difference between Mengzi and Xunzi is in focus and emphasis.

All of that said, it remains true that Xunzi's view of initial human nature is bleak. Why is it so bleak? Recent psychological research on assessments can shed light on this. It shows that how good or bad something seems can depend on a "baseline" in relation to which it is assessed. The baseline may well be implicit and not consciously factored in the assessment. A dramatic instance of this is that when we lose something—call it X—the loss of X is likely to seem much more negative than the acquisition of X had seemed positive.[5] We may not have had a baseline in relation to the acquisition of X. But when X is lost, the baseline of life with X is firmly in mind and the loss is felt as negative in a salient way.

If we view initial human nature in relation to a baseline that centers on our most persistent motivations (most of which are self-interested), it can look hopeful, as it did to Mengzi. We may be self-interested, but not entirely. Something perhaps can be built on this. If, on the other hand, our reference point is the motivations of civilized and refined people, it can look negative. It certainly did to Xunzi.

The next question, in relation to Xunzi's position, is how to explain the fact that some people—starting out as warped barbarians—become civilized, really good people. Any criticism of Xunzi can focus on the difficulty of arriving at an acceptable ultimate answer to this question. There is an immediate answer, though, that has considerable plausibility. The unruly two-year-old can improve through the advice and control of parents and teachers and become a sort-of-good adolescent or young adult. Confucius (see Chapter 4) provides the rest of the answer from this point on: it includes the inspiration provided by the *Book of Songs* (sometimes referred to as the *Book of Odes*), the shaping that results from ritual, and the inner harmonizing that is promoted by the right kind of music.

Xunzi talks mainly about ritual. We need to remind ourselves that ritual (which many of us associate with boring, slow-moving events) is a kind of social dance. It develops in us a familiarity with harmonizing our thoughts and movements with those of others. A great many brief events in everyday life, such as holding a door open for another person or thanking someone for a favor, can be put under the heading of ritual.

These are civilizing events. Holding a door open for another person is a more complex thing than one might think. First, it requires having an awareness of another human being moving through space. Not everyone consistently has this awareness. Occasionally one glimpses people who seem to move about as if they are the only people in the world. This is a kind of self-involvement that it is good to grow out of, just as it is good to have awareness that the world is shared.

Second, to hold a door open for another person is a tiny act of kindness. It is so tiny that the kindness is bound to seem trivial. But multiplied by hundreds or thousands of similar acts, it does amount to psychological self-training. One learns (and perhaps becomes habituated to) being a helpful person.

Thanking someone for a favor also looks rather trivial. How meaningful it is will depend not only on the importance of the favor but also on the tone of voice and the attitude with which thanks are uttered.[6] A number of such acts can amount to learning the emotion of gratitude. Occasionally you may encounter people whose emotional repertoire seems not to include that emotion. Any of us, though, will be a better person and have better relations with others if we have learned gratitude.

Adding all of this up, we can see that the Confucian account of how some people become refined and deeply good can provide an immediate explanation of how such goodness does exist in the world. But we also can begin to see why an ultimate explanation is more difficult. The situation is akin to that in causal explanations of how the world exists as we know it. After we have explained the causes of what now exists, we then need to explain the causes of those causes, and then the causes of the causes of the causes, and so on. Eventually we get to the question of first causes. There is a well-worn argumentative path on which some philosophers (including Aristotle and St. Thomas Aquinas) have arrived at the claim that God must exist, as the first cause of the universe.

What then is the first cause of refined and civilized behavior? How did those who taught the people who taught the people from whom we learned socially harmonized behavior (and also how to be grateful) acquire *their* degree of goodness? There is, of course, more than one possible answer to this question, and elements of answers can be found in Chapters 8, 9, and 10. In Chapter 8 we will examine Thomas Hobbes' account of the social contract, which—if one accepts it—could account at least for some starting points in the process of moral refinement. In Chapter 9 we will discuss Bishop Butler's and David Hume's pictures, which would have been congenial to Mengzi. Chapter 10 will point toward a different approach, rooted in Immanuel Kant's emphasis on moral reason.

The question for now, though, is how Xunzi (who holds none of these views) could explain the ultimate first cause of civilized refined goodness. It is clear that there had been a buildup in the past of the social structures of refinement and of genuine goodness. This is very important to Xunzi. If we ask the question "How is it that there are deeply good people in the world?" the first thing that Mengzi would have said is that there is an innate element of benevolence in normal human nature and that this sometimes is built upon. Definitely the first thing Xunzi had to say is that ritual and other developed social structures enable some of us to move toward being deeply good people. (He also would insist that this is an incremental process.) But then we can ask how these social structures originated. It may not be immediately clear what Xunzi's answer would be.

Here are two possible lines of thought—although it must be conceded that neither probably solves all problems. One builds on the idea that there have been very gradual developments of what we think of as civilized practices and attitudes. These could have taken on meanings as they ramified, which moved the process forward.

This line of thought can be appreciated in relation to the problems of social contract theories, such as that advanced by Thomas Hobbes. A social contract includes structures of loyalty to systems of law and also established morality. Hobbes in effect claims that it is *as if* our remote ancestors made such an agreement. It is far from clear to him that there ever was such an explicit agreement. One alternative then to any story of an explicit agreement is that there was a gradual expansion of cooperative behavior that deferred to what increasingly were recognized as implicit norms. Being semicivilized made human relations easier and safer, and increasingly caught on, as later did patterns of civilized behavior. Xunzi could have arrived at a story like this, and in fact there is a case for thinking that it is close to his story.

The other line of thought that Xunzi could have adopted is not inconsistent with the first. When we describe people, it is tempting to describe them as they definitely are—right now. But perhaps part of the story of what anyone at a given moment is like should be that person's potentialities or tendencies to develop in a certain direction.

The Swiss psychologist Jean Piaget is best known for his studies of stages of conceptual development in children. Not every child, of course, develops to the same point. But all the same, there are normal stages for various ages, and developing through these stages could be held to be latent in most very young children. In much this way, part of human nature could include a normal developmental path of increasing moral awareness—depending, as even Mengzi insisted, on circumstances and opportunities. Xunzi's bleak view of initial human nature could be consistent with something positive: a view of human moral development as it would occur in a context of civilized society. That there are civilized societies itself could be seen as the cumulative result of the normal human tropism, in moderately favorable circumstances, toward increasing refinement. We sometimes lean toward goodness as plants lean toward the light. Cumulatively, this will be a leaning toward increasing refinement.

This is an interpretation that I have developed elsewhere, and it is only a suggestion.[7] Xunzi did say something that points in this direction, though. He remarked that "In every case, people desire to become good because their nature is bad. The person who has little longs to have much."[8] In other words, whatever initial human nature (as immediately displayed) is like, there is a normal tropism toward something better.

What seems clearly true, as one of the conclusions of this chapter, is this: Mengzi's optimistic-sounding and Xunzi's negative-sounding accounts of human nature are not as opposed as they at first seem and indeed are opposed mainly in what they emphasize. Many readers may think that each of these philosophers has helpful suggestions in explaining how refinement and deep virtue came to be human possibilities. This can be consistent though with the view that it still remains a problem.

Notes

1. There are some useful overviews of early Confucian philosophy. See P. J. Ivanhoe, *Confucian Moral Self-Cultivation* (Indianapolis: Hackett Publishing Co., 2000). See also a collection of sizeable excerpts from early Chinese philosophical texts (with introductory commentaries): *Readings in Classical Chinese Philosophy*, eds. P. J. Ivanhoe and Bryan W. Van Norden (Indianapolis: Hackett Publishing Co., 2003). Three of the six philosophers represented (Confucius, Mengzi, and Xunzi) are Confucians. Van Norden has translated all of Mengzi: *Mengzi* (Indianapolis: Hackett Publishing Co., 2008). References to Mengzi in what follows will be from this. For a magisterial study of Mengzi, see also Kwong-loi Shun, *Mencius and Early Chinese Thought* (Stanford: Stanford University Press, 1997).

2. It is hard to be sure whether Hume had as much expectation of shared benevolent behavior as what Mengzi suggests. Hume certainly did insist that there were judgments based on benevolence that would be widely shared. His one example of a moral choice of behavior that would reflect shared benevolence centered on gout (a common disease in the eighteenth century that involved painful sensitivity in the feet). Hume claimed that if a man suffering from gout were walking toward you, hardly anyone would step on his feet rather than move out of the

way. See *Enquiry Concerning the Principles of Morals,* ed. Jerome Schnee-wind (Indianapolis: Hackett Publishing Co., 1983), p. 47.

3. An exceptionally good treatment of the difference between an occasional attitude and a systematic one has been provided by the nineteenth-century German philosopher Friedrich Nietzsche. Many readers would not immediately associate Nietzsche with benevolence, although it is worth mentioning that he suffered his final mental break-down while throwing his arms around a horse that was being beaten. He certainly was a strong advocate of systematic attitudes in life.

This comes out in his remarks on the problem of weakness of will (the problem of how people fail to do what in some sense they know is best). He observes

> *Weakness of the will:* that is a metaphor that can prove mislead-ing. For there is no will, and consequently neither a strong nor a weak will. The multitude and and disgregation of impulses and the lack of any systematic order among them result in a "weak will"; their coordination under a single predominant impulse results in a "strong will": in the first case it is the oscillation and the lack of gravity; in the latter, the precision and clarity of the direction.

See *The Will to Power,* trans. Walter Kaufmann and R. J. Hollingdale (New York: Vintage Books, 1968), pp. 28–29; italics Nietzsche's.

4. Martin L. Hoffman, "Interaction of Affect and Cognition in Empa-thy," in *Emotions, Cognition, and Behavior,* eds. Caroll E. Izard, Jerome Kagan, and Robert B. Zajonc (Cambridge: Cambridge University Press, 1984), pp. 103–131.

5. Cf. Paul Rozin and Ed Royzman, "Negativity Bias, Negativity Dominance, and Contagion," in *Personality and Social Psychology Review* 5 (1999): 296–320.

6. See *Analects,* 1.8.

7. See "Xunzi: Morality as Psychological Constraint," in *Virtue, Nature, and Moral Agency in the Xunzi,* eds. T. C. Kline III and Philip J. Ivanhoe (Indianapolis: Hackett Publishing Co., 2000), pp. 89–102.

8. Xunzi, trans. Eric Hutton, in *Readings in Classical Chinese Philoso-phy,* p. 287.

Questions for Further Consideration

1. When Mengzi speaks of innate benevolence, does this imply that any human being can be expected to do the right thing in any life-or-death decision?

2. Xunzi presents a less-positive view of human nature than Mengzi does. Does this imply a basic sinfulness in every human being?

3. Is the difference between Mengzi's view and Xunzi's that Xunzi emphasizes culture and the changes it produces more than Mengzi does? Or is there a more complicated difference?

Recommended Further Reading

Kwong-loi Shun, *Mencius and Early Chinese Thought* (Stanford: Stanford University Press, 1997) is magisterial and thorough. Two excellent collections of essays are Xiusheng Liu and Philip J. Ivanhoe, eds., *Essays on the Moral Philosophy of Mengzi* (Indianapolis: Hackett Publishing Co., 2002), and T. C. Kline III and Philip J. Ivanhoe, eds., *Virtue, Nature, and Moral Agency in the* Xunzi (Indianapolis: Hackett Publishing Co., 2000).

Chapter 7

The Christian Doctrine of Original Sin: Essential Human Imperfection

The doctrine of original sin includes a claim about human nature: that humans are all imperfect in their virtue. There are various explanations of how this imperfection happened to become a feature of human nature. It is important to appreciate these explanations, but in the end our concern will be to examine the view of human nature.

Original sin is often associated with the sin of Adam, when he ate the apple in the Garden of Eden. It is sometimes thought that all of his descendents (that is, all of us) inherited his sin in the form of moral imperfection. Further on in the Old Testament, there is a related thought about the sins of the fathers burdening their descendents. Besides these two biblical sources, there is an entirely secular basis for the doctrine, which needs to be considered.

Adam's sin in eating the apple and disobeying God is treated in the Bible as extremely grievous. It results in the expulsion from paradise of Adam and Eve and their having then to live by the sweat of their brow. Any twenty-first-century reader who takes the story at face value might be tempted to find the drastic punishment disproportionate to the offense. The usual reply to reactions of this sort is that God's reasons are beyond human comprehension. In the book of Job, God is reported as saying just this. It then would look like a kind of extreme arrogance to question what God decides to do.

There also are various nonliteral ways of understanding the story. It can be seen as a "just so" story, offering a narrative to explain a basic fact of human life—that often life is not easy, and we need to work. It also can be taken as a portrayal of a loss of innocence. The apple is fruit from the Tree of Knowledge. Knowledge has its costs and leads to a more complicated life than that of the simple hunter-gatherer.

The aspect of the story or legend of the Fall that is our present concern is this: it has been thought that included among the things we inherit from our ancestors are the blame and burden attached to what Adam did. Clearly, we have inherited having to live by the sweat of our brows. But the suggestion is that we also have inherited a kind of moral imperfection.

This idea is reproduced, but in an odd way, in an episode in the story of Noah's activities after the great flood. Once the flood waters receded and the possibility of normal life was restored, Noah planted a vineyard. He then made wine out of the grapes. The next step (as reported in Genesis 9: 20–27) was that he got drunk.

His son Ham happened to venture near where Noah was lying down naked. He saw his father naked. This presumably was inadvertent on his part but all the same violated a major taboo. Ham made the offense worse by going to tell his brothers what had happened.

His brothers, Shem and Japheth, knew how to behave properly. They took a cloak and walked backward, with the cloak behind them, so that the cloak lay upon Noah and covered him before they turned around and saw him. There is a wonderful twelfth-century fresco of this in the church of St-Savin sur Gartempe in France.

When Noah sobered up, he issued a curse. This is where the story becomes a bit odd. The curse, one might think, would be on Ham, who violated the taboo. Many twenty-first-century readers might think, in fact, that there should not have been a curse at all. What Ham did, after all, looks inadvertent; and in any case Noah brought about the problem and ought to have been ashamed of himself.

Still, the curse, as reported in Genesis 9.25, was not on Ham. It was instead on Canaan, Ham's son (and Noah's grandson), who it is said will be a "servant of servants."[1] Canaan had done nothing to create this mess. All the same, the curse in effect insists that Canaan inherited Ham's fault. It also makes it sound as if what is said of Canaan will apply to his descendents.

Whenever this story, including the curse, was inserted into the Bible (which contains material from various dates of composition), it was very convenient. The ancient Hebrews under Joshua are described as waging war to conquer and dispossess the Canaanites. Reading the story of Noah's drunkenness and subsequent curse, one is supposed to realize that in a sense the Canaanites deserved this.

The convenience of Noah's curse actually has had a long history. It has been said that in the bad old days before the civil rights movement gained traction, some racist preachers in the South used it for their own purposes. They deliberately misread the Bible, presenting the curse as one on Ham, and conjoined this misrepresentation with the assumption that Ham was the ancestor of the African peoples, including of course African Americans.

This is not the end of biblical presentations of the curse on the descendents of those who have sinned. In a stunning reversal (Jeremiah 31:28–30), Jeremiah reports that God is annulling any rule that sins are inherited. Specifically God says that "They shall say no more, The Fathers have eaten a sour grape, and the children's teeth are set on edge. But every one shall die for his own iniquity: every man that eateth the sour grape, his teeth are set on edge."

Original Sin and Human Imperfection

The remainder of this chapter is concerned with human psychology and with the place of a doctrine of original sin in relation

to human psychology.[2] Matters of faith and of the interpretation of religious texts are not a major concern of this book,
which in the end is more focused on philosophical issues that
can be argued and clarified apart from one's religious commitments. The information in the previous section about the religious background in the Bible of the doctrine of original sin
has some use. It places the doctrine in its original context. All
the same, the doctrine can be evaluated on its own merits.

Let me suggest then that there is a strong case for regard-
ing the doctrine, in one interpretation, as basically true, apart
from any religious uses that might or might not be made of it.
In another interpretation, it can seem questionable. Even so,
it could serve as a corrective to excessive confidence in human
virtue.

In presenting this case, a number of distinctions need to
be observed. One is between there being a strong case, on one
hand, and there being proof on the other. There also is a distinction between rigorous psychological studies on one hand, and
the observations of human beings made by perceptive people
on the other. We also need to consider a distinction between
moral lapses and lapses that might not be put under the heading of morality.

The contrast between having a strong case and having proof
is a prompt for caution. You can be justified in believing something on the basis of a strong case while bearing in mind that
there might be an outside chance of an occasional exception.
That you have not encountered an exception does not mean that
there cannot be one. This leads to some openness of mind.

Popular wisdom holds that "to err is human," and probably
the vast majority of readers believe this—and believe it on the
basis of what seems true of them and of everyone they know
well. But can we be sure that there are not some unusual people
who are entirely innocent and pure, who are exempt from original sin? Saints might seem like obvious possibilities.

It would be handy, in assessing this, if saints had written
candid and detailed autobiographies, giving us crucial evidence
in this form. The one saint who comes to mind who did
provide written detail of his life is St. Augustine. However, the

Confessions of Saint Augustine is in some ways driven by doctrine. A major point of the early part of the narrative is that St. Augustine had embodied the truth of the doctrine of original sin. He did things that were wrong and then over time worked to make himself better.

This does not prove that there are no exceptions, although it does (at a minimum) give the impression that you might have a hard time finding one. One reason is that even decent, well-meaning people can make mistakes, including mistakes about the nature of what they are doing. Someone may think that what he or she is doing is helpful and kind while in fact interfering in people's lives and making things difficult for them. We might think afterward that such a person was at fault: they may have meant well but all the same should have been more careful and more hesitant about entering the territory of other people's lives.

Some philosophers have thought that something like this kind of failing is a greater risk for people who are zealously virtuous than for those who are decent in a quiet and steady way. This view comes out in a sardonic passage in the Chinese Daoist classic the *Chuang-Tzu/Zhuangzi,* written in the fourth century BCE. Toward the end of the second chapter, Chuang-Tzu observes that virtue is like the warmth of the sun and mentions that once ten suns had risen over the earth.

This may seem to the casual reader like a conventional praise of virtue. But it refers to an ancient Chinese myth about the era in which there was a ten-day week and correspondingly ten suns, which took turns rising over the earth. One day all of them rose at once. The heat was intense, and the earth was in danger of burning up but was saved by the superhero archer Yi, who shot out nine of the ten suns.[3]

The sardonic point here seems to be that excessive virtue (something that goes well beyond ordinary decency) can be toxic. Whether one thinks that this is true or not, an obvious point is that many of our actions that affect other people can have ramifications that may not be immediately clear, so that someone who is well intentioned and wills only what is good still might on some occasions do some harm. In some of these cases, we might think that he or she should have known better or at least should have been more careful.

Even so, there might be people who simply are pure. We may not know any of them. But that hardly proves that they do not exist.

All the same, it looks extremely plausible to hold that, at the least, most people (and perhaps almost all people) have some failings or failures. There are influential psychological studies that appear to support that judgment. The best known are the Milgram experiment (discussed in Chapter 4) and the Stanford Prison Experiment.

Recall that in the Milgram experiment, subjects were told that they were participating in an experiment on learning. There was someone on the other side of a glass partition who was said to be a subject (but really was an actor), and experimental subjects were instructed to give him what they thought were electric shocks of increasing severity if he made mistakes. The actor made lots of mistakes, and in various iterations of the experiment most subjects continued (as they thought) to administer electric shocks, past a level marked dangerous.

In the Stanford Prison experiment, subjects were randomly divided into pretend-guards and pretend-prisoners in a simulated prison. The "guards" rapidly became abusive, and the "prisoners" soon began to exhibit the beginnings of psychological damage. Consequently, the experiment had to be cut short.

These experiments are often cited to support a bleak view of human virtue. They also feature in the "situationist" school of psychology. This school contends that the situations in which people find themselves typically play a major role in how they behave and that any stable character that one might think someone has is likely to play a lesser role.

There clearly is something to this, although there is debate among psychologists as to how much. With regard to the subject of this chapter, though, it should be noted that a significant minority of subjects refused to go along with the Milgram experiment. And there is no reason to suppose that if the Stanford Prison experiment were repeated, every subject would behave badly.

One thing that situationist psychology arguably gets right is that someone who behaves well in one kind of context could very well behave badly in another kind of context. This parallels the belief many of us share (in what might be termed "folk psychology") that people are sometimes at their best and sometimes at their worst. The thought also is that if you know someone well, you will know the kinds of situations in which that person tends to be at his or her best and the kinds of situations in which you would have lower expectations for that person.

Are there many (or any) entirely pure people, devoid of "sin"? Here the distinction between rigorous psychological study and informal reports of experience becomes important.

One could imagine a psychological study that rigorously followed the lives, in great detail, of a large number of people to see if they were always pure. Such a study, of course, might not be feasible. It also would amount to spying, and for this and other reasons it would violate the ethics guidelines that were developed after the Milgram experiment. It is likely that the experience of many perceptive people would suggest that entire purity is not to be found. But this, while it does promote skepticism about entire purity, is hardly proof that it never (or even that it very rarely) occurs.

Further, we have to consider what is to count as "sin." In recent centuries, philosophers and laypeople have tended to distinguish moral judgments from normative judgments that we would not normally classify as "moral." One way of seeing the separation is to ask of some bit of bad behavior whether one would term it "immoral." We might well condemn insensitive remarks that gratuitously hurt someone's feelings, but we would be unlikely to label them as "immoral" unless they did major damage. Murder, rape, and theft, though, clearly are immoral.

John Stuart Mill in particular pursued this distinction, first in a brief passage (the fourteenth paragraph of Chapter 5) in *Utilitarianism,* and then at length in *On Liberty.* What we think morally wrong, he says, is what we think should be punished, either legally or through guilt feelings (on the part of the person who misbehaved) or through social pressure. His tendency in *On Liberty* is to suggest that there is poor behavior (e.g., behavior that is foolish or tasteless) that can occasion our avoiding and perhaps even admonishing a person but does not justify aggressive pressure on the offender. This heavy pressure, Mill thinks (with some qualifications), should be reserved for behavior that directly harms someone who is not a consenting adult. The word *harm* should be understood here as involving significant damage.

Should the "sin" in "original sin" be construed as any clearly faulty behavior (including insensitive or inconsiderate actions) or should it be construed more narrowly as immoral behavior? If the answer is the former, then it is hard not to believe that everyone at some time falls short. This still does not amount to proof of a doctrine of original sin, but the case looks strong.

Suppose however that "sin" is interpreted as immoral behavior. Suppose also that Mill's rather narrow guidelines for what should count as immoral are accepted. In assessing the content of these suppositions, the reader should realize that one implication of Mill's position is that premarital sex in which no one is directly harmed (although in some cases it might be criticized in various ways) would not count as "immoral."

If these interpretations are accepted, the doctrine of original sin can look less thoroughly plausible. Are there people who, even if they are not perfect, have not murdered, raped, stolen, committed other acts of dishonesty, or inflicted other kinds of serious damage on innocent persons? It is hard not to believe that there are many people who have never done any of these things.

There might be a separate issue if someone who had never done anything immoral had, however, been tempted. Does this count as a manifestation of "original sin"? The reader can make up her or his mind on this.

Let me suggest though that our judgment could be split. Temptation to do something that is morally wrong arguably is evidence of imperfection. But it is also arguable that by normal standards anyone who has never done anything morally wrong has a perfect record of morally acceptable behavior and in this respect counts as having moral rectitude. This suggests the following conclusion.

The doctrine of original sin looks extremely plausible if it is taken as a claim that human perfection is never, or almost never, to be found. If it is taken as a claim that entire moral rectitude is never to be found, it may be more questionable. Even then—even if in this interpretation the doctrine is questionable—it might serve as a useful corrective for those who are excessively optimistic about their fellow human beings.

Notes

1. Wording in references to the Old Testament in this chapter is drawn from the King James translation.

2. Let me report my debt, in thinking that there is a "naturalistic" interpretation of original sin that is very plausible, to a talk given by Herbert Fingarette many years ago at a conference.

3. The relevant passage can be found in Chuang-Tzu. *The Inner Chapters,* trans. A. C. Graham (Indianapolis: Hackett Publishing Co., 2001), p. 58.

Questions for Further Consideration

1. How are we supposed to respond to the idea that what we are is marked by "original sin"?

2. Are some people exceptions to this doctrine, or does it apply to everyone?

Recommended Further Reading

The Bible is strongly recommended as relevant to an understanding of original sin. A book about a major pioneer of the idea of original sin is Eric Osborne, *Tertullian: First Theologian of the West* (Cambridge: Cambridge University Press, 1997).

Part III

SOME MODERN VIEWS

Chapter 8

Hobbes (and Some Darwinian Echoes)

Thomas Hobbes, whose working life was in the seventeenth century, had a view of human nature embedded in his pioneering account of the social contract. A social contract might be thought of as a tacit agreement among the great majority of members of a society. What they agree to would include respecting legitimate authority, obeying a set of laws enforced by that authority, and also observing moral standards.

Why would people agree to all of this? Part of Hobbes' answer concerns what people are like. We are self-interested and generally tend to measure our well-being in comparison with that of other people. We have appetites for various things and want them not to be snatched from us. More generally, we want security, both of life and limb and also of property. Our strong sense of self-interest causes us to favor a social order that protects us and that does not favor other people to our considerable disadvantage.

As background to this, it is worth mentioning Hobbes' life as a "loner." He was not an academic philosopher but rather earned his living by serving as a tutor or companion to sons of aristocratic families. This included being tutor to Prince Charles (the future King Charles II) in exile in the wake of the English civil war (in which Puritans led by Oliver Cromwell defeated the royal forces).[1] His first job had involved teaching mathematics to the son of the Duke of Devonshire. As music was thought akin to mathematics, part of the job was to play the lute and sing on suitable occasions.

Hobbes' main philosophical project was to explain, and in a way also to justify, something that was already the case: the social contract. People who lived in civilized societies (such as England) by and large acknowledged legal and moral constraints on the kinds of things that they could do. They also by and large acknowledged the authority of the political and legal apparatus (including kings, queens, judges, magistrates, and officers of the law).

The legal and moral constraints with which Hobbes was concerned were mostly designed to minimize acts that threatened other members of the society or their well-being, property, or security. People who have grown up in a civilized society often may feel that they have, as it were, signed up not to harm others in such ways, and also by and large to obey the laws and the major moral requirements that are generally agreed on. These are not precise commitments.

There can be exceptional cases in all of these areas, and also someone who has a sense of having "signed up" to adhere to established law and morality might claim an exception in cases in which it is doubtful that this is justified. Further, there will be a fair number of people whose loyalty is not very steady and some people whose loyalty is really rather slight. All the same, in Hobbes' England (and in America today) there is a general sense that most people usually can be counted on to adhere to established law and morality and that our lives are more secure as a result than they might have been otherwise.

This understood general (or almost general) agreement can be thought of as like a contract. The thought is that we are obligated not to do certain things to other people in much the way we would be obligated if we had signed a contract that committed us not to do those things, in exchange for the promise that other people would not do those same things to us. This is a social contract in the sense that the agreement is widespread within a society.

Nevertheless, none of us has signed such a contract. Nor did our parents or grandparents. In this respect the social contract might look like a fiction. Hobbes is quite aware of this. He has what amounts to two fallback stories to save the idea of a social contract. One fallback story is very dramatic. The other is undramatic but subtle.

The dramatic story is set considerably in the past, when human beings lived in what Hobbes calls a state of nature. Imagine a world without law, without the organizations that allow for political authority, and without any clear sense of morality. Cavewomen and cavemen would be able to get food and other very bare necessities in such a world, and perhaps most of them could survive. But—absent law and morality—anyone's food or fur coverings could be stolen by others. Competitors could be wounded or killed. Projects that involved work for the future would be precarious in that everything could be ruined or seized at any moment by interlopers. To experience anything like this today, you would have to live in a war zone. When Hobbes says that in the state of nature life would be "nasty, brutish, and short," virtually all readers would agree with him.

Besides the nastiness and the risks of bodily harm and death, this primitive world would be devoid of the things and experiences that require considerable preparation over time. What would be the point of such preparation if anything can be taken away or destroyed? A first thought might be that, after all, some people are much stronger than others and that these people at least would have security. But even strong people are vulnerable when they sleep, or can be ganged up on and overpowered by a group of weaker people.

In short, the self-interest of virtually everyone in a state of nature is to have arrived at an agreement that creates constraints on various forms of harmful behavior. People do not always adopt policies that are to their own (or anyone else's) interest. But self-interest sometimes does carry the day. Apparently it did in our escaping the savage world of the state of nature. We now (as least most of us) have the strong sense of living in societies governed by what amounts to social contracts.

But when were such social contracts (or some first social contract) agreed to? The image of primitive people arriving at and subscribing to, an agreement is appealing; but did it ever happen? A plausible reading of what Hobbes wants to say is that in the end he is unwilling to posit an actual occurrence at which a social contract was accepted. The claim rather was that it is *as if* a social contract had been agreed on.

This is not as dramatic as an actual initial agreement on a contract would have been, but it does represent a subtle analysis of what now exists. It also should be mentioned that there is another subtle account of how we have a social contract. It is one that appears not to conflict with Hobbes' analysis and indeed fills it out. David Hume, in the eighteenth century, suggested the model of two men rowing a boat together.[2] (People dancing together also would provide a model.) Those who are carrying on the joint activity might not exchange words about what they are doing. But they very likely are continuously adjusting their activities to those of the other person or persons. Eventually it will come to seem as if they had agreed to perform in a coordinated way, even though what is involved is a gradual adjustment rather than any overt agreement.

In any event, let us look at Hobbes' idea that we are living as if there had been a social contract. Whether we accept this story or cling to a more dramatic story in which there was an actual initial agreement, it looks like our having a social contract (instead of living in a state of nature) had to be motivated. It isn't a random development. What is the motivation?

Hobbes' answer is clear. The motivation is a sense of personal self-interest. Any rational being would come to realize that her or his life would be better in a civilized society than in a state of nature and thus will be motivated to arrive at mutual understandings with others.

In any explanatory account a positive element (what is claimed to explain the facts) will stand out. But a negative element (something denied or ignored) also can be quite noticeable. It can be striking that certain things are left out of the explanation. In Hobbes' case, what is left out is initial concern among primitive humans for the safety and well-being of some other people, such as family members. Also not to be found in

Hobbes' account is any sense that as a social contract takes hold we do come to care for some of the people we live among.

There is a Sherlock Holmes story in which the crucial clue is not something that happened but rather something that did not happen. Someone had gone past the family dog in the night, and the dog did not bark. This was an important clue to the identity of the person who passed near the dog.

If we look merely at Hobbes' positive account of the social contract, we may miss a feature that made Hobbes' view seem peculiar and unacceptable to some of the philosophers who followed him. This is the absence of any sense that one motivating factor in the development of human societies is people's sympathy, benevolence, or caring directed toward others in the society. This could be seen as an absence of something that should have been there. It plays a large role in the rejection (explicit or implicit) of Hobbes' account by the two philosophers to be presented in the next chapter, Butler and Hume.

Butler and Hume especially reject the view of human nature that is implicit in Hobbes' account. Here is a reconstruction of Hobbesian human nature: Human beings by and large are appetitive, self-interested, and competitive. They want various things for themselves, and above all they want their lives to go well. They also do not want other people to flourish at their expense. The combination of these traits leads to some defensive attitudes in life. We are constantly aware of dangers and competitive pressures, which include a great many things that could go wrong because of other people. The ideal then is an environment in which we are protected against most or all of these things.[3]

Some of this is extremely plausible. The apparatus of law and established morality to which most of us at least largely subscribe surely owes much of its appeal to our desire for protection and security. Let us put this desire in perspective. Many writers on values have contended that the most positive things in life loom less large than the most negative ones. If this seems doubtful, try this thought experiment. Imagine that you have a choice between two weeks of ordinary life, or instead a week of the best experiences you can imagine followed by a week of the worst experiences you can imagine. (You can reverse the order of these if you like.) Which would you choose? My guess is that the vast majority of readers would prefer the two ordinary weeks to the two weeks of extremes, because the badness of the very bad will seem to outweigh the goodness of the very good.

Some of the worst things that we can imagine happening to us have little direct connection with other people. Terrible diseases and injuries would be on this list. But what we would fear also would include torture, extreme humiliation, being deprived of any control over our lives, extreme isolation, and having everyone and everything that we care about destroyed. These are experiences that some people actually have had, if they were targets in a genocidal campaign or were caught in a war zone (especially if the war was conducted without any agreed-on restraints).

To consider all of this is to realize how much we prefer to live in a situation in which the kind of social contract that Hobbes spoke of is operative. It is hard to dissent from his view that human beings who are not totally stupid—and in particular are able to look ahead—would want and would support such a contract. They also would be (or at least should be) disturbed and apprehensive if there is any weakening of the social contract.

Our primary concern here, however, is not with the social contract but rather with the view of human nature that Hobbes deploys in his account of it. Are human beings like what Hobbes described? Has he discovered the foundations of human life and interactions?

Are Virtually All Human Beings, in Their Essential Nature, Appetitive, Self-Interested, and Competitive?

The word *virtually* is in the heading of this section because of the difficulty of ruling out the existence of extremely unusual human beings. This imposes a limitation on theories of human nature. It often is tempting to say "Any human being will . . ." or "All human beings are. . . ." But it looks like such claims can be undermined by the discovery of someone who is extremely peculiar, who does not seem to have normal human attitudes or interests. Such a person may have been damaged in some way or may be genetically abnormal: there can be a variety of explanations for the differences from the rest of us. It always may turn out, though, that the peculiar person is at some level less different than one might at first think. All the same, we have to be open to the thought that plausible generalizations can have occasional exceptions.

The question of whether virtually all human beings are (in their essential nature) appetitive, self-interested, and competitive is complicated in another way—one that already has been gestured at. It asks whether almost all of us are governed by appetitive and self-seeking desires. But also there is the implicit question of whether this is the whole story. Has something else been left out?

One reason why this is important is that none of those who came after Hobbes and criticized his views denied that appetitive and self-seeking desires play a major role in the lives of almost all of us. In short, there were no philosophers who argued that Hobbes was *entirely* wrong. Butler and Hume certainly did not. My guess is that most readers might think that even if Hobbes was one-sided in his account of human nature, he did get some things more or less right. Who among us is not influenced by appetitive, self-seeking, and competitive desires?

This perhaps should be qualified in two respects. It may be that Hobbes made the role of competitive instincts in our lives seem greater than it sometimes is. There are clear examples of competitive behavior in schools, careers, and in such spheres as entertainment and sports. But it is easy to get an impression from Hobbes that competitive urges are central in life. Given his account of the state of nature, one can see how plausible this would be. However, it might be argued that in modern everyday life there can be a fair number of people in whose lives it is not central. These people might be moderately secure, not markedly ambitious, and sufficiently satisfied with what they have that they are not bothered by the fact that some other people have more.

Another point at which the centrality of appetitive, self-seeking, and competitive desires might be challenged is this: it can be claimed that there are people in whose lives self-seeking desires play only a small role. Some of these are of the type that we refer to as saintly. They are not "out for themselves" but devote themselves to the needs of others.

This possibility is worth bearing in mind. But let me (for what it is worth) defend Hobbes on this point. It is hard to arrive at any certainty about the inner thoughts and motives of people who are regarded by the world as behaving in a saint-ly way. All the same, it looks clear that the thought that one has been behaving in a saintly way would be very gratifying indeed. In some cases, being saintly—to put it crudely—could be an ego trip. It may be that some saintly people, whose virtues include that of humility, would be among the first to say such a thing; and surely there is nothing wrong with such innocent satisfactions.

A parallel move can be found in the ethical writings of Immanuel Kant (to be discussed in Chapter 10). Kant devel-oped a system of ethics in which morality was held to center on a sense of duty in upholding valid principles. However, his view of human nature included a sense of self-regard that is impor-tant to most (or nearly all) people, and he remarked that there was no case to be found in which someone did the right thing *only* from a sense of duty. "Dear self," he says, will enter in.[4] The reader realizes, with a mild shock, that Kant is including his own moral choices among those that turn out not to be purely motivated by a sense of duty.

Part of what I have been trying to suggest is that even some-one who believes that Hobbes' account of human nature is not entirely correct can still believe that there are some important truths in it. This also suggests the possibility that variants of Hobbes' position could have some appeal and that the model of appetitive, self-seeking, and competitive humans can be extended to groups of organisms. This brings us to the Darwin-ian echoes of something a little like a broadened version of Hobbes' view.

Darwinian Versions of Human Nature

Anyone who has read accounts of Darwin's life, which was marked by other-regarding concerns, could be confident that Darwin would not have entirely endorsed Hobbes' account of human nature. It also should be said that Darwin's theory of natural selection could lead to various views of human nature, including some that Charles Darwin himself probably would not have shared. A degree of clarity may be possible in outlin-ing the views of a single philosopher that would not be possible in canvassing an entire school of thought. Nevertheless, we can say a little about tendencies that were encouraged by Darwin's scientific work.

The first thing to note is that there is some resemblance between the competition among groups of organisms that is crucial to the process of evolution and the instinctive competi-tiveness that Hobbes located within human nature. One of Darwin's early admirers, Herbert Spencer, coined the phrase "survival of the fittest," which then found its way into later editions of Darwin's *The Origin of Species*. One can see the survival of the fittest at work in a telling exhibit in the Museum of Natural History in London of peppered moths collected in Manchester in the late nineteenth century. As industrial activ-ity led to more smoke and soot in the air, the colors of the moth wings became (apart from any contribution from smoke and soot) appreciably darker. This gave the naturally dark-winged moths the advantage of blending in with their surroundings (including tree trunks and branches), thus becoming less visible to birds who might eat them. Dark-winged moths became the fittest, surviving and successfully breeding more often than lighter-winged competitors.

It has been suggested that a major influence on Darwin was the work of an Anglican clergyman, Thomas Malthus. In his *Essay on the Principle of Population* (1798), Malthus argued that organisms have a tendency to multiply geometrically when resources increase arithmetically, thus actually putting more strain on resources and leading to more competition for survival. This would be true not only of human beings but also of other organisms.[5]

The variation through time of the influence of ideas like Malthus' should be noted in passing. It lent itself, in Victorian England, to the idea of surplus human population. Readers of Dickens' *A Christmas Carol* will remember that Scrooge excuses his initial reluctance to give to charity by referring to the surplus population.

Readers of John Stuart Mill's *On Liberty,* on the other hand, may be struck by his insistence in the final chapter that some people have no right to marry and have children. He applies this to those who lack the resources to support their children adequately (and he treats marriage as the crucial decision, seeming to ignore the possibility that people might have children without being married). The argument for this position, which might strike some readers today as less liberal than he usually is considered, concerns competition for jobs. Contributing to the excess population in this respect harms others.

Finally, nowadays there are some people who see increasing human populations as a different kind of threat. Even if resources are somehow made available, the argument is that increasing populations will be connected with increasing strain on the environment. Much of the full impact of the harm that will result—including what stems from an increased pace of global warming—may be delayed. In other respects the anxiety here is comparable to Mill's anxiety about increasing populations.

Let us return to Darwin and those directly influenced by Darwin. Darwin's theory lent itself to the idea of a competitive struggle for continued existence among groups of organisms, such as the dark-winged and the light-winged peppered moths in industrial Manchester. It should be noted that in one obvious respect this image of life as a competitive struggle is reminiscent of Hobbes, and in another respect it is sharply different. It captures the idea that a part of normal life, including normal human life, is the attempt to protect oneself against hazards of various sorts, and that some methods of protection (including that of living in a society with a well-established social contract) can be better than some alternatives. On the other hand, Darwin's theory does leave room for the evolutionary advantage of altruistic traits.

Underlying this is a division between Darwin, on one hand, and Hobbes on the other. Hobbes focuses on appetitive behavior and competition among individuals. Darwin focused much more on what amounts to a competitive struggle among groups of organisms. In this context altruism can have real advantages. Having said that, one also has to admit that some views influenced by Darwin then began to focus on what could be called social Darwinism, including a struggle among individuals to gain what is widely desired and to be secure in life.

Plainly there is more than one version of Darwinism. Daniel Dennett, in his *Darwin's Dangerous Idea*, takes pains to separate Darwin's version from some derivative versions. One such variant, which has an appealing simplicity, held that adaptation (with its competitive advantages) was in general brought about by (and represented) genetic change. It is clear that Darwin thought that this was sometimes the case, but clear also that he did not believe that it was always the case. Dennett cites passages in which Darwin insists that some feature of an organism (apart from any genetic modification) can become, over time, useful in ways that were not originally the case. As an interesting addendum he also quotes the German philosopher Friedrich Nietzsche, in his *Genealogy of Morality* (1887), making essentially the same point.[6]

One apparent implication of this is that what we might consider human nature could change drastically in the future, even apart from any genetic change. The need to adapt to radically different conditions might lead to different patterns of human nature. One can only speculate on what human nature on remote planets might be thousands of years from now.

Notes

1. Hobbes returned to England in 1652, while Cromwell was still in power. He held that the importance of respecting the power that maintains social order justifies submitting to the conqueror in a civil war. See *Leviathan,* ed. Michael Oakeshott (Oxford: Basil Blackwell, 1957), p. 461.

2. The convention that allows "stability" in the possession of external goods, Hume said, "is not in the nature of a promise." The two men rowing the boat together can reach an understanding even if no promises are involved. See Hume, *A Treatise of Human Nature,* 2nd ed., ed. L. A. Selby-Bigge, rev. P. H. Nidditch (Oxford: Clarendon Press, 1985), pp. 489–490.

3. Michael Oakeshott puts some of this very well in his introduction to Hobbes' *Leviathan.* The existence of others of one's kind is an impediment in the pursuit of felicity "for another man is necessarily a competitor" (op. cit., p. xxxiv). Hobbes in the final section of *Leviathan* (p. 460) remarks that "there is a perpetual contention for honour, riches, and authority."

4. Immanuel Kant, *Grounding for the Metaphysics of Morals,* 3rd ed., trans. James W. Ellington (Indianapolis: Hackett Publishing Co., 1993), p. 20.

5. Cf. Jonathan Howard, *Darwin* (Oxford: Oxford University Press, 1982), pp. 14–15. Howard speaks of Malthus' empirical generalization "being taken entirely out of its original context in 1838," and supplying Darwin with the idea of "the struggle for existence which forms one of the cornerstones of the theory of evolution." Howard also, quoting at length from Darwin (including Darwin's assertion that "Natural selection will never produce in a being anything injurious to itself . . ."), observes that natural selection implies "selfish" organisms (ibid., p. 24).

6. Daniel C. Dennett, *Darwin's Dangerous Idea: Evolution and the Meanings of Life* (New York: Simon and Schuster, 1995), p. 465.

Questions for Further Consideration

1. Is Hobbes saying that no one really cares for anyone else, but in the end is just self-seeking. Or is he saying that, whether or not someone cares for other people, there will be a strong element of caring for herself or himself?

2. Would the existence of saints, who are willing to make sacrifices for the sake of other people, refute Hobbes' position?

Recommended Further Reading

Frederick Copleston, *A History of Philosophy*, vol. 2 (London: Burns Oates and Washbourne, 1959) includes a reliable account of Hobbes. An outstanding recent book is Quentin Skinner's *Hobbes and Republican Liberty* (Cambridge: Cambridge University Press, 2008).

Chapter 9

Butler and Hume:
Inherent Tendencies toward Altruism

Bishop Joseph Butler and David Hume are two major philosophers who flourished in Britain in the eighteenth century and who both disagreed with Thomas Hobbes. The reader will recall that Hobbes, as presented in the preceding chapter, held that human nature was self-seeking and competitive. There was no suggestion in Hobbes' writing that human beings also generally have a benevolent or altruistic element in their thinking.

Neither Butler nor Hume would have denied that human beings often do exhibit self-seeking and competitive elements. But Butler, and Hume later, denied that this was the whole story, and in fact insisted that something very important was left out of Hobbes' account. Butler provided an inspiration for lines of thought that developed this point. Hume early in his career expressed admiration for Butler.[1]

There clearly were some differences between the two. For one thing, Butler was a Protestant bishop and Hume soon became known as a "freethinker" in matters of religion. Also, Hume's account of human sympathy and benevolence is more complex than anything corresponding to it in Butler's philosophy. But they did to a considerable extent agree on human nature and on what they thought Hobbes missed.

Butler's most impressive line of thought centered on what has been widely thought to be a conflict in human motivation.

113

This involves an opposition between, on one hand, self-interested behavior and, on the other hand, behavior motivated by concern for others (and perhaps designed to contribute to their well-being). It seems obvious to a great number of people that these are opposing forces.

Behavior motivated by concern for others is often spoken of as "altruistic." It is important to realize that *altruism,* like many of the terms used to describe human motivations or behavior, has a range of meanings connected with degrees of concern. A very strict standard for altruism (in the strongest sense of the word) would require that everyone's well-being counts equally in one's thought and motivation. This would imply entire unselfishness: anyone's well-being would count for as much as one's own. It also would imply lack of partiality for friends and loved ones, including parents, siblings, and one's children.

This possibility comes up sometimes in discussion of utilitarianism, an ethical philosophy pioneered in the eighteenth century by Jeremy Bentham and developed in a sophisticated form in the nineteenth century by John Stuart Mill. There are now many forms of utilitarianism, but they all share an emphasis on a balance of favorable consequences over unfavorable ones. This is held to be the ultimate test of the actions we should choose, or the rules we should follow, or the policies we should adopt. What is recommended is whatever is likely to result in the most favorable balance of good consequences over bad ones.

How is this to be reckoned? The answer is by adding up the values obtained by any sentient creatures (including animals) that will be affected and subtracting the negative values. Given this method of decision, we might well think that everyone's values or well-being should count equally in the calculation. In other words, the simplest form of utilitarianism (a theory that has many complicated forms) would insist that, at bottom, we all be thoroughly unselfish and also not partial to our loved ones. This has been regarded as creating a problem. It is thought by the vast majority of people (including the vast majority of utilitarians) that thorough unselfishness and lack of partiality simply goes against human nature.

This could be used to argue that if there is anything to be said for utilitarianism, it cannot be the simplest form of utilitarianism. Richard Brandt, whose utilitarianism was not simple, dramatized this with a couple of deliberately odd examples. In one, a man promises to pay a teenager for mowing his lawn but then (after the lawn has been mowed) decides that doing something else with the money would have better consequences. In another, a man who has been saving money for his children's college education decides that, from an impartial point of view, it would be better to give the money to comparable students of the same age who have higher College Board scores.[2] Most readers will think that such decisions sound inhuman, and Brandt of course agrees with them. The examples are produced to make the point that utilitarianism cannot be simple and cannot endorse complete impartiality in life.

In other words, extreme altruism is counterintuitive, except perhaps for saints who are dedicated to very unusual sorts of lives. This still leaves open the possibility of moderate altruism, which involves a concern for the well-being of others (including one's loved ones) that is more than occasional but not all-consuming. It also is consistent with a moderate degree of favoritism for one's loved ones. You could reasonably favor them over strangers in such matters as giving presents, but arguably not (if you are a member of a hiring committee) in deciding who gets a job. Clearly, there is an even more modest degree of altruism, which involves occasional concern, perhaps a little more concern than the average person has.

Still, it may well look as if there is a conflict between altruism (of whatever degree) and self-interest. Again and again it would seem we have to choose between our own well-being and that of others. A moderate altruist, out of the goodness of his or her heart, would not always make the same choice. Rather, on some occasions, one would pursue one's own well-being, and on others one would pursue that of others (at one's own expense).

Butler rejects the thought that there is a general opposition between altruism and self-interest. Before explaining his views, let me remark on Butler's peculiar position in the history of philosophy. He would be unlikely to appear on many lists of the ten most important philosophers. But—in a discipline in which oppositions of contending views are the norm—he has a distinctive achievement. He argued for a counterintuitive position, and his argument I think has been very widely accepted, with rather little dissent.

Butler's View of Altruism and Self-Interest

The opening move in Butler's *Sermons* is to question what it is that we should consider self-interest. Bear in mind that what people want, and think is good for them, may not be good for them in the way that they think. Psychologists for example have shown that, while people who already have a good deal of money may think that it would be very good to have more, getting more money typically makes only a slight difference to their level of happiness.[3] Our wanting something does not imply that it will benefit us significantly, and in some cases it may not benefit us at all or may turn out to be personally damaging.

On the other hand, what is in our self-interest often does have a connection with what it is that we care about. If we are quite indifferent to something, it is usually the case that getting it will not make any difference to the quality of our life, especially if we remain indifferent to it after we have it. Because of this, any investigation of what is really in our self-interest should begin, Butler thinks, by asking what the sources of our satisfaction could be.

Clearly, some of these sources will be the object of purely self-interested motivations. Wealth, prestige, and popularity are obvious examples. We want them for ourselves. People usually think that if they attain such things, their lives will be better. Empirical evidence (as in the case, just mentioned, of well-off people getting more wealth) sometimes suggests a more skeptical judgment.

But then cases vary; and the degree that is desired, of whatever it is, also can make a difference. People who have moved from poverty to some degree of wealth usually do seem to have better lives. Writers and artists who have been ignored may well be happier, at least in the short run, if their work gets more attention and respect. Prestige and respect, though, seem to be like wealth, in usually offering diminishing marginal returns. It may be that past a certain point, the degree of attention and respect will not make much difference to the felt quality of life. Almost everyone wants more, and then still more, but that does not mean that more always will make a significant positive contribution to one's life.

Butler's point about such purely self-interested sources of satisfaction is this: They may well contribute something to the quality of our lives. However, there is a built-in limitation to what they can contribute, in that they constitute a rather narrow base for personal fulfillment. It will generally be the case that people can do better if their personal fulfillment has more sources, resting on a broader base.

Sources of happiness and fulfillment, for many people, include other areas of concern besides such things as wealth and prestige. In particular, caring about other people—if all goes well—can be a major source of happiness and fulfillment. Caring about the arts, about a sports team, or about the well-being of people far away (whom one does not even know) also can enrich a life, especially if things go at least moderately well.

To put the point crudely: if we remain largely within ourselves in our concerns, life will be experienced as narrow and at best moderately satisfactory. If, on the other hand, we have interests and concerns that take us out of ourselves, the chances for a really satisfactory life become greater. Many, although not all, of these concerns outside ourselves, will involve people whom we care about. They will be altruistic concerns. But it will be in our self-interest to have them.

Hence, other-regarding concerns can be both altruistic *and* self-interested. There is no essential conflict between these two categories. The other-regarding concerns will not be *purely* self-interested. But, all the same, they can matter considerably to the quality and satisfaction of someone's life, and an intelligent person will welcome and pursue such concerns.

None of this was part of Thomas Hobbes' view of human nature. Hobbes appears in some respects to have been a "loner" and concentrated on matters that would involve pure self-interest. Bishop Butler, in his discussion of the sources of personal fulfillment, clearly was giving people advice about how to live. But he also was crafting a criticism of Hobbes' account of human nature as containing some truths but also leaving out things that were important.

This also represented a criticism of Hobbes' account of the origins of the social contract. Hume developed in some respects a similar criticism. As we will shortly see, he also developed a complex account of human nature that was closer to Butler's view of things than it was to Hobbes'.

Hume on the Social Contract and on Human Nature

The reader will recall that Hobbes portrayed the social contract as a widespread implicit agreement to be governed by an apparatus of law and order, and also to be governed by an established morality. In his account, he suggested that it was *as if* people realized that it was in their self-interest (if they wished to avoid lives that were nasty, brutish, and short) to adhere to this compact. Pure self-interest was at the root of the social contract.

Hardly anyone would deny that intelligent self-interest supports the social contract. But is it a matter of *pure* self-interest? Hume denied that it would be. Even in the imagined "state of nature," the primitive state that would have preceded a social contract, people would have had families, and could be expected to have affection for the members of their families. A plausible image of the development of what we think of as a social contract would include the fact that the participants would have motivations that included affectionate regard for significant others. They also might be supposed to have got along reasonably well with at least some other people (rather than there being some constant war among people).

What we might think of as a social contract could have developed gradually from such relationships. Hume asks us to imagine two men together rowing a boat. What the two are doing should be coordinated, but it seems ridiculous to imagine a constant dialogue in which each says to the other, "Now put your oar there, while I put mine in such-and-such a place." Rather it is a well-known phenomenon that people can adjust to each other in their movements, without explicit communication. In much this way, people who get along reasonably well can create (by gradual steps) what amounts to a social contract.

Hume regarded affectionate regards for some, and perhaps more broadly a degree of benevolence and sympathy, as normal parts of human nature. Before we explore Hume's views, and the philosophical context in which they were developed it might be useful to say a little about Hume's own nature—as background to his philosophy.

Hume was like Hobbes in never marrying or having children. But, whereas Hobbes seemed to be a loner, Hume (at least in his maturity) was widely considered amiable and very sociable. One can get a sense of his personality from his writings. At one point Hume speaks of the importance of "mutual deference" in human relations.[4]

There is a relevant story about Hume in an amply contextualized edition of James Boswell's *Life of Dr. Johnson* (of dictionary fame). Hume was widely attacked as a religious skeptic. At one point Hume asked the bookseller Cadell, who was his publisher, to invite to dinner Hume's most severe critics and to invite Hume also. The account afterward of the meeting quoted one major critic, Dr. Price, as saying that "they all loved David."[5]

Hume's view of human nature was that it included an element of benevolence or sympathy for others. In this (as was mentioned in Chapter 6) it was remarkably like the position taken two thousand years earlier by the Confucian philosopher Mengzi (Mencius), whose philosophy Hume was extremely unlikely to have known about. Like Mengzi, Hume did not maintain that benevolence was the dominant attitude in human life, nor did he deny that purely self-interested motivations are typically a good deal stronger.

All the same, Hume argued that there were clear manifestations of widespread benevolent attitudes. Like Mengzi before
him, he was aware that some individuals seem never to have a
benevolent thought. Again like Mengzi, he thought that such
cases could be discounted because, in effect, they could be
explained away. If it is true that the emperor Nero was volun-
tarily cruel, this was because his disposition had been perverted
by circumstances.[6] In effect, he had lost his humanity.

As Chapter 6 spelled out, Mengzi's position was very much
oriented toward practical and political concerns. His hope was
that rulers, if they could be led to come to terms with their
own occasional benevolent impulses, would then broaden their
benevolence and practice good government. Hume's emphasis
on the widespread occurrence of benevolent or sympathetic
judgments, in contrast, was linked to a theoretical puzzle.

The puzzle was this: Suppose that we reject Hobbes' account
of the purely self-interested origin of the social contract, and
suppose also that we agree that Hobbes was only half-right
about basic human selfishness. All the same, it has to be conceded that self-interested concerns dominate most people's behavior most of the time. How then can we explain the prevalence
and power of moral judgments, in which such self-interested
concerns are not supposed to play a major role?

In what follows, we can examine Hume's link between his
view of human nature and his reconstruction of the origins
of morality. His argument had a significant influence on the
image of morality entertained by philosophers who came after
him. This includes Immanuel Kant, whose view of human
nature (very different from Hume's) will be examined in the
next chapter.

What Makes Morality Possible

The power and usefulness of morality, Hume thinks, can be
understood only if one realizes that there is an element of
benevolence in human nature. There is "some benevolence,

however small, infused into our bosom." This enables one to "depart from his private and particular situation" and "to chuse a point of view, common to him with others."[7]

Even a small bit of benevolence can establish common ground with others. However different we are from other people, we will share this with them. This in Hume's view is a basic fact. "Let a man's insensibility be ever so great, he must often be touched with the images of RIGHT and WRONG, and let his prejudices be ever so obstinate, he must observe, that others are susceptible of like impressions."[8]

This connects with a point to which Hume devotes much argument: that if we analyze people's moral judgments, we find that considerations of usefulness generally carry considerable weight in determining what is morally approved. Further, the usefulness can be to strangers or to people in general, and generally is not restricted to what is to our own benefit. Indeed, approval that is based on the usefulness of something to oneself will normally not be thought of as *moral* approval and also would be extremely unlikely to be something that most other people would concur with. In all determinations of the morality of specific practices, Hume holds, "public utility is ever in view." We ascertain "the true interests of mankind."[9]

Hume does concede that an account like that of Hobbes' captures part of the reason why we tend to favor what promotes the general utility. But he denies that "*all* moral affection or dislike" arises from such an origin. There is, he insists, a "general affection for virtue" that plays a part.[10]

Here is one way to reconstruct the picture that has been briefly summarized. We humans, self-seeking though we are, also are social animals. We normally have particular affections, but even beyond this we tend to like getting along with (and communicating with) the people around us.

To say "What I really want is X" does not usually create or strengthen a bond with the people around us. We often do have desires or strong preferences. But even though these will loom large in our lives, talking about them rarely will engage other people, apart perhaps from people who already care a lot about us.

What works best in communicating with others is to talk about common interests. Here is one interest we are virtually certain to have in common with the people around us. We would normally like not to have dangerous and disruptive things happening around us. This can be explained in large part by reasons that Hobbes had explored. But part of the explanation is also the bit of benevolence that exists in almost all of us. All things equal, we would prefer not to see people hurt.

Not surprisingly, even if our benevolent motivations turn out to be weaker than our purely self-interested ones, they will represent common ground. Discourse within this common ground can agreeably bring us closer to other people.

This, as Hume sees it, is the origin of morality. The initial motivational base of morality may not seem very powerful. But once morality (so to speak) gets going, it can exert a great influence on people who become used to morality-talk. Social reinforcement has a great deal to do with this. One product then, as Hume says, is a growing "general affection for virtue."

Hume's account of human nature anticipates Kant's (the subject of the next chapter) in one respect. It starts from an established phenomenon of human thought (namely the prevalence of moral thought and judgment) and relates this to basic human nature. The two accounts differ significantly. But both trace a connection between sophisticated structures of thought and behavior and what it generally is to be a human being.

Notes

1. See Earnest Campbell Mossner, *The Life of David Hume* (Oxford: Clarendon Press, 1970), pp. 74 and 110.

2. Richard Brandt, "Toward a Credible Form of Utilitarianism," in *Morality and the Language of Conduct*, eds. H.-N. Casteneda and G. Naknikian (Detroit: Wayne State University Press, 1963).

3. See Michael Argyle, *The Psychology of Happiness* (London: Methuen, 1987).

4. *An Enquiry Concerning the Principles of Morals,* 2nd ed., ed. J. B. Schneewind (Indianapolis: Hackett Publishing Co., 1993), Section 8, p. 68.

5. See James Boswell, *Life of Dr. Johnson,* vol. 2, ed. George Birkbeck Hill (New York: Harper and Brothers, 1891), p. 505, n.2.

6. See *An Enquiry Concerning the Principles of Morals,* Section 5, p. 48.

7. Ibid. Section 9, p. 74; Hume's spelling of "chuse."

8. Ibid., Section 1, p. 13; emphasis Hume's.

9. Ibid., Section 2, p. 19.

10. Ibid., Section 5, pp. 39–41; emphasis Hume's.

Questions for Further Consideration

1. Butler was after all a Protestant bishop. Was his main contention that we are unselfish because we would like to be able to go to heaven? Or is his main point different from this?

2. Hume believes that it is to your advantage to be a virtuous person. Why? If you could fool everyone all the time about what you were like, would that undermine his argument?

3. If in fact none of us is perfect (because of original sin), would that undermine Hume's argument?

Recommended Further Reading

Useful views of Butler and of Hume are to be found in Austin Duncan-Jones, *Butler's Moral Philosophy* (Harmondsworth, England: Penguin, 1952); and V. C. Chappell, ed., *Hume: A Collection of Critical Essays* (Garden City, NY: Doubleday and Company, 1966).

Chapter 10

Kant: The Need for Reason to Dominate

Immanuel Kant lived in Königsberg, in what then was Prussia, in the eighteenth century. His insistence that reason should dominate might remind some readers of Plato. But the context of their philosophies differs greatly and gives Kant's emphasis on reason an entirely different quality from Plato's.

Plato's vision of governance by reason was in the direction of personal life and also in the governance of a community. Kant certainly had things to say about both topics. But reason played the largest and most conspicuous role in his analysis of morality. Thinking rationally, in his view, was the central feature of being moral.

Kant's emphasis on reason in human nature has a great deal to do with a particular conception of morality, in which laws are basic and desires for personal happiness count for very little. The importance that Kant thought reason has can be appreciated only in the context of his systematic approach to philosophy.

The first step is to appreciate his characteristic method. The second is to understand how it is (in his view) that one's personal happiness counts for next to nothing in morality. The third step is to recognize the special importance, in Kant's view, of laws. Given all of this, we can see why Kant regards reason as crucial to human life.

Kant's Method

Let us look first at Kant's characteristic method in his large works. The starting point of his three Critiques was a set of obvious facts about human thought and experience. The first Critique (the *Critique of Pure Reason*) started from familiar facts about the structure and form of human experience of, and thought about, the world. The second Critique (the *Critique of Practical Reason*) began from facts about the structure and form of moral thought. Finally, the third Critique (the *Critique of Judgment*) began from, among other things, the form and characteristic assumptions of aesthetic experience and judgment.

Another kind of philosopher—someone like Kant's predecessor Rene Descartes—might then have looked for ways of validating the assumptions built into these forms of experience and thought. Kant in contrast treated them as givens. They were ingrained in human thought prior to any validating experience or any empirical investigation, and in that sense were a priori.

Kant's move was to investigate what was implicit in the structures and forms of human thought. Some basic truths about the world as we experience it then would turn out to be valid because they are inherent in human thought and represent a kind of built-in structure of whatever we could experience in the world—a structure contributed as it were by us.

In other words, these basic truths about the world might seem to capture characteristics of the world, but really what they capture is the framework of our experience and thought. It is because of this that they are not really empirical. One example of such truths is that every event has a cause. Some features of the conservation of matter (unless, of course, matter is converted into energy) also would have this character.

The philosopher W. H. Walsh very cleverly illustrated these a priori truths that could be known to be true before any empirical testing. Imagine being in a car that suddenly stops. "Why did it stop?" we ask the driver. Suppose the reply is "For no reason at all." Or suppose that something disappears from our room. "Where did it go?" we might ask. A reply might be "Nowhere—it simply vanished into thin air."

We can reject both of these answers out of hand. Things (such as the car's suddenly stopping) do not happen for no reason at all, and items do not vanish into thin air. We know this not because we happen never to have experienced such things before but because we have a sense of the structure of what we can experience. This tells us that the car's suddenly stopping has to have a cause—events have causes—and that a suitably qualified claim of the conservation of matter is a priori true. We know all this before any empirical investigation.

At this point we need to look closely at two complications. Kant was keenly aware of one of them. He seemed oblivious to the other.

One complication is this: if we are looking for a universal structure of a priori truths, we have to consider the possibility (perhaps the likelihood) that nonhuman beings (including any intelligent nonhuman beings) would have a framework of experience different from ours.

Some of Kant's early work was in astronomy, and he might readily have been able to imagine the possibility that some of the stars we see have planets that are inhabited by intelligent beings that are not like us. This may well have played a part in some striking passages in the *Critique of Pure Reason*. In one passage he remarked that there is "no need to limit this kind of intuition—intuition in space and time—to the sensibility of man. It may be (though we cannot decide this) that any finite thinking being must necessarily agree with man in this regard." In another passage he said that "Even if different forms of intuition (from space and time) and likewise different forms of understanding (from the discursive form of thought or of cognition through concepts) were possible, yet we cannot think them up and make them comprehensible in any way."[1]

What Kant said suggests that communication with such thinking nonhumans might well be difficult if not impossible. The twentieth-century philosopher Ludwig Wittgenstein made a related claim. He observed that "If a lion could talk, we would not understand him."[2]

That there is a framework generating a priori truths is, Kant thought, also true in relation to morality. It is clear, though, that he would reject any suggestion that a valid extraterrestrial morality would be different from ours.[3] Intuitively, it might seem that the practice of morality implies a much stronger claim of universality than that implicit in ordinary experience. Kant remarked specifically that all rational beings (which includes any nonhuman thinking beings) are obligated not to lie.[4] Even if Kant is right about all of this, all the same, it is interesting to speculate on what we could say—that would be cogent—if a group of technologically advanced and seemingly much more intelligent nonhumans arrived on our planet and began killing humans for fun.[5] Would this antihuman behavior be morally wrong, and if so can we contrast it to human hunting of less intelligent animals? These are, of course, highly debatable questions.

It is worth emphasizing that although Kant made moral claims that we might regard as controversial, he scrupulously acknowledged that he had not *proved* anything. Rather (here, as in his treatment of space, time, and the categories), he has merely shown some implications of what is already part of the structure of our thought. In this case, the crucial starting point is our concept of morality.[6]

The Categorical Imperative and Laws

Kant's view is that morality at its most basic level takes the form of laws, and this is embedded in the very structure of moral thought. We can think of laws as general statements of what we should do or of what we should not do. Such laws, in Kant's view, would apply to any rational being and (like the laws of physics) would not allow of exceptions.

This view emerges starkly in two passages in the *Grounding of the Metaphysics of Morals* (the *Grundlagen*). The first of them insists that the categorical imperative (which is a statement of basic principle that is the foundation of morality) has objective necessity and carries with it the necessity of law. A second passage observes that at the heart of this is the universality of law, to which the maxim (the motivating statement of the sort of thing that should be done or should be avoided) of an action should conform. This gives us the concept of duty.[7]

Why did Kant assign laws this central role in morality? This question brings us to the complication to which I want to argue Kant was oblivious. This has to do with variations among traditions of ethical thought. If the starting point for Kant was a pattern of thought and experience, then it matters if not all human traditions of ethical thought have the same pattern.

Within some of these traditions there is a widespread sense that morality at its most basic level takes the form of laws that govern our conduct. In others this feature is largely absent. We can begin to examine this variation by looking at Kant's view of what morality is, and of the importance in morality of laws. Then we can look at some variations among ethical traditions, including at least one that Kant knew quite well.

Some of the constraints that Kant thought are built into morality can be appreciated in relation to a fundamental distinction he drew between hypothetical imperatives, on one hand, and the categorical imperative on the other. A starting point in understanding Kant's view of the structure of morality is to realize the importance of its not being "hypothetical."

Hypothetical imperatives have an "if" clause. They recommend what you should do *if* you have certain goals or interests. Most of your goals and interests will be in some sense personal: they will not be shared with absolutely everyone. Kant contended that there is one goal though that is universal. Everyone, he thought, wants happiness.

One might think at first that even if almost all goals and interests vary widely and are personal, the shared desire for happiness could be the basis for a universal element in an ethics. However, as Kant maintained, this is not the case. Even if everyone wants happiness, what would make you happy might be quite different from what would make one of your friends happy. The content of what is involved in being happy is thus indeterminate. In this sense, there remains an "iffy" element in strategies for achieving happiness.

Also, Kant was not inclined to think that being happy usually has some kind of great value. He saw nothing wrong, in general, with trying to become happy. But in cases in which the drive for happiness conflicts with morality, happiness is to be spurned. He also remarked that the search for happiness in fact tends to diminish contentment.[8] In any case, happiness (in his view) is far less important in life than whether you are a thoroughly moral person.

We can put this in perspective if we compare Kant's ethical philosophy with that of Aristotle, whose view of human nature was examined in Chapter 5. Aristotle and Kant do share some things, including a sense that reason must be central in human life as it should be lived. But much of Aristotle's major work on ethics, the *Nicomachean Ethics,* is to a large degree concerned with the factors that would enable someone to achieve *eudaemonia*. This Greek word is best translated as "well-being" but also often translated as "happiness" and definitely has connections with both happiness and human flourishing. Aristotle believed that a good life would include, among other features, some degree of happiness. Kant, in contrast, believed that the search for happiness has at most only a minor role in how we should live.

If morality is not primarily a search for happiness, then what is it? Kant considered two features of morality to be essential. One is that it is prescriptive in a very pressing way. That is, morality tells us how to behave, and how not to behave, and does this in a way that would normally be expected to be taken quite seriously. There are other prescriptive systems that are much less pressing. Etiquette for example tells you which fork to use when eating a salad and how to address a thank-you note. But lapses normally would not provoke strong condemnation. Moral lapses, on the other hand, typically are taken to call for serious social pressure, and often it is expected that the person who misbehaved will have feelings of guilt.

The second feature of morality that Kant regarded as essential is that its recommendations represent an orderly system resting on laws of good behavior, rather than being a miscellaneous collection of demands. The categorical imperative, he observed, is concerned "with the form of an action and the principle from which it follows."[9] Duty, a concept to which Kant assigned great weight, "is the necessity of an action done out of respect for the law" (by which Kant here means moral law).[10]

Laws, it should be noted, have a role in many forms of knowledge. Laws of nature were a large part of the discoveries in Sir Isaac Newton's physics. Newton's achievements had enormous prestige and seemed to a great many people (including Kant) to represent a model of what real knowledge might be like.

There also are laws, in any advanced society, that govern what kinds of behavior the government will or will not allow and what kinds of punishment a violator should expect. Finally, there may be moral laws that require or forbid certain forms of behavior. Some of what is contained in the moral laws may find its way into the laws that are enforced by the government. In our society, for example, there is considerable overlap between the crimes that are most severely punished and the actions that are widely considered to be morally wrong in the most gross way. Nevertheless, the most general enforcement of morality in a society will be by means of social condemnation of miscreants along with encouraging them to feel guilty.

It may seem obvious that morality centers on laws that stipulate sorts of behavior that can, or cannot, be allowed. Most readers will regard this as obvious because of a dominant tradition of moral thought in the Western world. This tradition goes back to the Ten Commandments in the Old Testament, which consist of laws that specify behavior that is required or is to be condemned. That morality is rooted in such generalizations is something that has entered into common sense. Thus we often speak of a good person as "a woman (or man) of principle."

However, as noted in Chapter 4, judgments of behavior in some societies and traditions, including ones that many people would respect highly, often exhibit a different structure. This is especially true in classical Chinese philosophy and in at least some important classical Greek philosophy. The differences of these from what most of us think of as a dominant tradition are striking, and might be taken to undermine Kant's model of ethics.

One difference can be mentioned in passing. It concerns a distinction that we sometimes make between behavior that falls within the purview of morality (and which if faulty is immoral) and behavior that lies outside the realm of morality. This distinction is best understood if we briefly look at the structure of ethics.[11]

If ethics is the study of how people can best lead their lives, then it includes not only what we generally refer to as "morality" but also judgments of what would be most rewarding in life and also judgments of how best to conduct personal relations in a congenial way. It is quite possible for us to think that someone has ridiculously shallow ideas of what is most rewarding in life, without for a minute thinking that such a person is immoral. Equally, we do not consider someone to be immoral just because she or he tends to be a bit insensitive and sometimes hurts friends' feelings. Not all faults are moral faults.

The distinction between morality and other kinds of normative judgment has been a staple of Western thought since the time of Kant. We might think of it roughly as a distinction between on one hand, actions someone might perform (such as murder, theft, swindling, or doing grievous bodily harm to another) that are society's business and on the other hand actions (that may be foolish or tasteless but do not amount to direct harm to anybody) that we regard as the agent's own business. It is easy to think that we can isolate and examine the morality that is dominant in any other society.

Perhaps so. However, many scholars of classical Chinese philosophy have concluded that there is no word in classical Chinese that can be translated as "morality." In effect, then, there is no conscious division between morality and other parts of ethics. In the thought of, say, Confucius, all of ethics is a seamless web. Some scholars of classical Greek philosophy have made a comparable claim about ethics.

Even if all of this is granted, though, it is highly arguable that there are certain problems and judgments that Confucius or Aristotle treated in the same way we treat moral problems and judgments, even if there is no special word or concept associated with these problems and judgments. Confucius, for example, took a very strong negative view of rulers or officials who worsened the lives of poor peasants by selfishly increasing their taxes or by thoughtlessly conscripting their labor at just the time when they needed to be working in the fields. The force of Confucius' judgment is one that we would associate with a moral judgment. Something similar holds for Aristotle.

If it is agreed then that there are morality-like elements in the Confucian tradition and in that which includes Aristotle, what about laws of morality? The answer here is less simple and also less positive.

Confucius and Aristotle had what can be termed a hybrid ethics. Both insisted that a great many ethical choices (including some that we would regard as moral) have to be made on a case-by-case basis, with due regard to the particular features of each case. This is central to Aristotle's treatment of the mean in the *Nicomachean Ethics*, and to the flexibility that Confucius spoke of in *Analects* 18.8 (in referring to questions of when a government is bad enough that a conscientious official should resign).

In short, most of what an extremely good person (in both Aristotle's and Confucius' accounts) would judge should be done or not done would not derive from anything like laws. However, this is not true of 100 percent of such judgments. Aristotle said that there are certain things that never should be done and gave the examples of adultery, theft, and murder.[12] This certainly makes it seem that there are at least a few law-like generalizations that Aristotle accepted. Arguably, Confucius also accepted some law-like generalizations, although in his case the formulation of specific examples is less easy to find.

Kant certainly was familiar with Aristotle's ethics. Indeed, he decried the fact that Aristotle included the hypothetical imperatives of the search for *eudaemonia* in an investigation of how we should behave in life. Clearly Kant could not have liked Aristotle's insistence that many of the choices involved in finding a mean had to be attentive to the particular features of the case at hand (and hence could not be derived from, or appeal to, anything like a law).

The important thing in our discussion though is this: Kant may have wanted to think that the centrality of laws in morality is like space and time and the categories in our experience of the world—that is, a source of essential truths that hold for everyone. However, this does not fit Aristotle at all well. It is much more plausible to hold that space, time, and the categories are universally part of the structure of human experience than it is to maintain that moral laws have a comparable role in all human moral thought (let alone all moral thought among thinking beings).

Reason in Morality

Reason or rationality enters into morality, in Kant's account, in a number of respects. We can start with the primary formulations of the categorical imperative. One of these is that a choice is morally acceptable if and only if one could acceptably will that behavior of that sort be a universal law. There are two ways in which a choice could fail these tests and be revealed as immoral. It would fail if it would be impossible for there to be a world in which everyone behaved in that way. Alternatively, it would fail if—even if it were possible for there to be such a world order—no reasonable person would want it.

An example of the first sort of failure is choosing to break a promise. There could not be a world in which everyone always breaks promises, because if this were the case, then the words "I promise" would lose their current meaning. Everyone would know that the words meant nothing, and hence there would no longer be any real promises.

The second sort of failure, Kant suggested, is exemplified by someone's choice never to help others in need. We all want to be helped if we are in need. Hence (in contemplating the possibility that we might some day be in need) we cannot will a world in which no one ever helps anyone else.

A number of things should be said about the form of the categorical imperative that centers on the requirement of universal law, before we move on to some other forms. One of the ways in which reason becomes crucially important in Kant's ethics is this: Suppose we are able to work out that a certain kind of behavior (and the maxim—i.e., the statement of motivating principle—that underlies it) could not be acceptably universalized, thus realizing that the behavior is wrong. Normally we would find this out through an exercise of reasoning.

A second point about this form of the categorical imperative is that it is enormously appealing. What it stipulates could be thought of as an insistence that it is not acceptable to behave in a certain way if, at the same time, you would not be willing to have everyone else behave that way. In other words, it refuses to countenance treating oneself as an exception to the moral rules. Intuitively, it does seem that a great deal of immoral behavior involves someone's treating herself or himself as an exception. It does look like Kant has captured something important.

The third point though is less positive. Arguably there are forms of behavior that fail Kant's test but that virtually any intelligent person would think are not immoral. Here are three examples. One, which I owe to Derek Parfit, is behavior that sometimes occurred when dueling (quite possibly to the death) was common. Imagine a man who deliberately fires his pistol into the air rather than trying to kill his opponent. Such behavior could not become universal, simply because if everyone supported this policy, dueling would lose its rationale and its meaning. There would be no real dueling and hence no instances of people deliberately firing their pistols into the air in duels.

This is, in formal terms, very like Kant's argument that breaking promises is morally unacceptable. But virtually anyone would agree that there is, at the least, a moral question mark attached to breaking promises (at least, breaking promises of some weight), but no moral problem at all with firing the pistol into the air.

In fact though, many instances of breaking promises (and also instances of lying, especially so-called white lies) might seem (if nothing of importance is at stake) trivial enough not to be subject to moral judgment. This connects with a possible objection to Kant's view of morality: that he, as it were, moralized a number of things that (even when they are not very nice) do not rise to the level of concern we normally connect with moral judgment. The two remaining examples—designed to undermine the moral requirement that universal practice of what is judged be possible and acceptable—follow this line of thought. One kind of behavior that fails Kant's test is being five minutes later than expected for an appointment. Another is realizing—after buying something and then moving some distance away—that you were given a few pennies too much in change but not doing anything about it.

Being five minutes later than expected simply could not be a universal law. If everyone were always five minutes late, then when you were supposed to be somewhere at 9:00 you would know that you were expected at 9:05, and so would have to appear at 9:10 to be five minutes later than expected. Anyone who has followed this line of thought could think "So then, I would have to appear at 9:15 to be five minutes later than people would anticipate." But there is no end to the regress of thought that all of this entails.

Running back to return the few pennies in change, on the other hand, could be a universal law. Further, insofar as moral issues are taken to be issues of principle, and there is a principle of honesty in handling money, it might seem that not to run back is a moral lapse. Let me suggest—and some readers may disagree—that it seems slightly foolish to run back if the amount of excess change is really tiny, and further that it is far from clear that there is anything in this case that calls for moral judgment. This represents a serious objection to Kant's construal of ethics, to the extent that Kant wanted to emphasize formal implications. What looks important in not returning the change, and also in being a few minutes late, is not the form of the relevant judgments but rather the degree of significance of what is at stake.

It may well be that someone sympathetic to Kant could, without much difficulty, modify Kant's theory of ethics to accommodate the problems that have just been raised. Kant certainly does at some points appeal to the importance of something as relevant to our moral approach to it. The most striking example is what he said about the regard due to persons (i.e., rational beings). A rational being, he insisted, represents something whose existence has in itself an absolute worth—an end in itself. Hence any rational being (even someone who has irrationally behaved very badly) has to be treated with respect and also should never be treated as merely a means to some goal (and not as an end).[13]

This requirement of respect for any rational being is an alternative form of the categorical imperative. It concentrates on a basic value rather than on the formal requirement of universalizability (i.e., of being able to be accepted as universal law). My sense is that in recent years the best Kant scholars, by and large, have preferred to emphasize this second form of the categorical imperative.

Yet another form of the categorical imperative in effect combines tendencies of the two forms that thus far have been presented. The combination centers on the idea of a Kingdom of Ends—a community or a world in which acceptable moral policies are universally accepted and in which every rational being is treated with respect. Admittedly, such an ideal community does not exist, at least on this planet. However, the ideal has a definite use. Even if others cannot be counted on, and may try to misbehave or to "free ride" on our responsible choices, we should behave *as if* we live in a Kingdom of Ends. This appeals to the intuition that it is immoral to treat oneself as an exception to acceptable moral requirements, even if others are doing this. This third form of the categorical imperative, like the first one, presumes that we are capable of rational thought in assessing what it would be like for a moral policy to be universal.

Like the second one, it presumes that we are rational enough to be able to value and respect rationality in others (as well as in ourselves).

Reason in Human Nature

There are two separate respects in which Kant thought that to understand the distinctive nature of morality is to realize the important role of reason in human nature. First, he believed that our awareness of the importance of laws in morality, along with the realization that a priori any law is universally valid, represents an exercise of rational thought. Reason enables us to accept only moral judgments that can be willed to be universal laws and to perform only actions in which rational beings are treated as ends and not merely as means.

The second respect in which reason is crucially at work in moral thought is quite different and requires more explanation. The reader will recall that Kant held that our experience of the world includes structural elements (such as space, time, and the categories) that were contributed by us rather than (as it were) coming to us from the world out there. The question naturally arises: what is the world like in itself, apart from the structural elements within which we experience it?

Kant's term for the world as we experience it (within the constraints of the structure contributed by us) is the "phenomenal world." The world as it is in itself, absent those elements contributed by the human mind-set, is termed the "noumenal world." God presumably experiences the noumenal world. We humans do not.

We not only can distinguish between the phenomenal world, which is largely accessible to us, and the noumenal world; we also can distinguish—with regard to anything—what it is like in phenomenal reality and what it is like noumenally. Thus we can inquire, of our own nature, what we are like noumenally. It might not have been entirely surprising if Kant had answered that we can know nothing of our noumenal selves. Instead his answer is that we can know virtually nothing.

What then can we know of the noumenal world? Kant approached his answer by pointing out that "the rational being counts himself, qua intelligence, as belonging to the intelligible (i.e., noumenal) world. . . . But on the other hand, he is conscious of himself as being also a part of the world of sense."[14] Our phenomenal nature includes various desires and inclinations, but presumably these are not part of our noumenal nature. A human must represent and think of itself, Kant said, "as intelligence, i.e., as independent of sensuous impulses in his use of reason (and hence as belonging to the intelligible world)."[15]

In other words, while we cannot as it were experience our noumenal reason, we know that it is there. It has to be there to cause the morally virtuous choices (independent of sensuous impulses). These are choices that we are aware of making in the phenomenal world.

Thus we can be aware of our use of reason in two distinct settings. One is entirely within phenomenal experience. Frequently we can find ourselves (in the familiar phenomenal world of ordinary experience) using reason to solve problems. Moral problems, in which moral laws play a major role, will be especially prominent in this.

Kant also thought, though, that you can infer that the noumenal you has reason, that is at the root of your moral capacities. Part of the argument for this is our sense of human freedom. "Freedom" like "reason," in Kant's account, can be used both to refer to a capacity (our ability to choose in a rational and free manner), and also to a realized capacity (your choosing rationally in a way that exemplifies your freedom).

The inference to a noumenal reason gets its strength from the following. Part of the structure of our moral thought includes moral responsibility, the assumption that we can be praised or blamed for our moral choices because we are free. Kant is what is sometimes called a "soft determinist." He believed, because of our a priori knowledge of cause and effect, that every moral choice is causally necessitated. But he also believed, because of our a priori awareness of moral responsibility, that every choice is free. The freedom, along with the reason that it embodies, is located then in the noumenal world.

This amounts to a final complication in this very complicated rococo philosophy. Relations of cause and effect that we can know about virtually all occur within phenomenal experience. There is one exception that crosses the boundary between noumenal and phenomenal reality. This is in the way we can infer that our morally virtuous choices were ultimately caused by noumenal reason.

Notes

1. See *Critique of Pure Reason,* trans. Werner S. Pluhar (Indianapolis: Hackett Publishing Co., 1996), B 72, p. 103, and A 230, B 283, pp. 294–295. A third relevant passage is A 42, B 59–60, pp. 94–95.

2. *Philosophical Investigations,* trans. G. E. M. Anscombe (London: Macmillan, 1953), Part II, xi, p. 223e.

3. See Immanuel Kant, *Grounding for the Metaphysics of Morals,* trans. James W. Ellington (Indianapolis: Hackett Publishing Co., 1993), #425, p. 33.

4. Ibid., #389, p. 2.

5. See my "Ethics for Extraterrestrials," *American Philosophical Quarterly* 28 (1991): 311–320.

6. See *Grounding for the Metaphysics of Morals,* #445, p. 48.

7. Ibid., #419–421, pp. 28–30.

8. Ibid., #395, p. 8.

9. Ibid., #316, p. 26.

10. Ibid., #399, p. 13.

11. Kant's distinction between morality and other forms of normative judgments is implicit in the distinction between the categorical imperative and hypothetical imperatives. Mill's distinction is briefly summarized in paragraph 14 of Chapter 5 of his *Utilitarianism.* His *On Liberty* can be read as a revisionary attempt largely (with some qualifications) to limit the realm of morality to judgments of behavior that harms people who are not consenting adults.

12. See *Nicomachean Ethics,* trans. Terence Irwin (Indianapolis: Hackett Publishing Co., 1999), Book 2, Chapter 7, no. 18, p. 25.

13. *Grounding,* #428, pp. 35–36.

14. Ibid., #453, p. 54.

15. Ibid., Third Section, #457, p. 57.

Questions for Further Consideration

1. What did Kant think is the connection between being rational and being virtuous?

2. Could Kant's view be refuted if someone could arrive at rational strategies for profiting from other people's misfortunes?

Recommended Further Reading

Two useful collections of essays on Kant are Paul Guyer, ed., *The Cambridge Companion to Kant* (Cambridge: Cambridge University Press, 1992); and Robert Paul Wolff, ed., *Kant: A Collection of Critical Essays* (Notre Dame: University of Notre Dame Press, 1967).

Chapter 11

Marx and Alienation: Our Flawed Participation in Life

Karl Marx lived in the mid-nineteenth century, when capitalism (the investment of money to make more money) had developed as an economic system, but there were dissident radical movements springing up here and there. His view of human nature was that it is most fulfilled when there is a balanced work life and also satisfactory connections with other human beings in general. As he saw it, a great many people in his time (in part thanks to the way capitalism had developed) experienced just the opposite of this fulfillment. Their economic life was one-sided, their work activity was both narrowly restricted and exploited, and divisions of social class kept them from the full range of human connections. Marx held that we need to understand human nature in terms of what gives us fulfillment or the reverse. Only then can we get a full sense, Marx thought, of what is deeply wrong with our society.

Marx's view of human nature can be understood best if we explore the range of his interests and get a sense of how his views of various areas of knowledge are connected. It scarcely need be said that Marx was not only an original thinker but also one widely thought to have had some wrong ideas. This view has become even more pronounced since the fall of communism in Russia and Eastern Europe, especially since this communism is usually regarded as a terrible failure. Marx's name has always been associated with communism.

His views and interests, however, are more complex than one might first think. He is best known as a political philosopher, one who advocated widespread revolts against established orders and who also advocated communism. As we will see, what he thought of as "communism" was quite different from what came to dominate Russia and Eastern Europe. It is clear that he would have been appalled by those versions of communism. All the same, Marx's history of the future—his prediction of how human societies would develop—looks very wrong. Some might argue, though, that the future is not finished, and there might be further developments that will change the picture.

Be that as it may, a basic point is that it is extremely difficult to find anyone in the history of the human race who was wrong about everything. Marx developed views on a variety of subjects, including basic human relations and also what can make life meaningful. It may turn out to be the case that Marx, even if he was sometimes very wrong, did get some important things right (or at least largely right).

Let me mention one thing in particular that those sympathetic to Marx think he got right. This is that social and economic arrangements play a major role in shaping the kind of people we are and the lives we lead. Many of us, most of the time, think of ourselves as individuals; and it is easy to think of our lives and personalities as crafted by us independent of the social and economic conditions in our society. Of course we all are individuals. But we would be very different individuals if we had grown up in the Middle Ages or in a society so very poor that hardly any work was available. A hundred years ago in America a great many people of the sort who now go to college were forced to forego higher education so that they could earn money to help their families make ends meet.

The general point is that our individual natures are not hermetically sealed from what the social and economic currents around us are like. Even if we rebel against some of these social and economic currents, they still will be reference points (whether positive or negative) in our personal development. Not only will they shape what we are, but they will also condition the opportunities that we have and the constraints we will be under.

To give a personal example: to have grown up in a middle-class family in Chicago instead of a poor family somewhere in Eastern Europe will remain an important factor in my life. The textures, opportunities, and constraints of middle-class life at that time made a large difference. So, too, did the kinds of career that were available to someone like me. In a very different society or a very different time, these might not have been possibilities. The reader may be able to think, in a comparable way, of how social and economic structures played a major role in shaping her or his life. If this is true, it is an important basic insight.

Besides his political philosophy and his history of the future, Marx produced considerable work on the economics of his day and also on human relations and potentialities. The role of the social fabric in our experiences and projects, and above all its effect on our sense of fulfillment, was central in all of this. Marx was very concerned with what he thought human beings need to have a good quality of life.

This brings us back to his view of human nature. It can be summarized as holding that human nature is such that our lives are marred by what Marx terms "alienation." He thought, conversely, that to be free of alienation is to have a good chance of having a desirable kind of life. In order to understand this view, we need to consider what he means by alienation. Also, because in Marx's view there is more than one form of alienation, we need to explore the varieties of alienation. We can examine his ideal of what life can be like once these forms of alienation are eliminated.

Alienation and Its Varieties

Here is one interpretation of alienation. It is a state in which something fundamental is missing, so that life seems incomplete or not balanced. It would be tempting to identify alienation with a psychological feeling—a sense of alienation—but that would be too simple. Often people do have a sense of something fundamental that is missing in life. But even when something fundamental is missing, often there is no sense of this—no feeling of loss or absence. Most of us are conditioned by what we are used to. We regard it as normal, and because of this we may never judge it or have a sense of its inadequacies.

Admittedly, we often think that life could be better. It would be nice to have more money, a better car, and more interesting vacations. But bear in mind that what Marx thought of as alienation is connected with something *fundamental*. It is something woven into the structure and texture of our lives. Missing more money and a better car hardly qualify at this level. Missing a supportive social environment or good opportunities for personal fulfillment would be much stronger candidates, in Marx's view, for counting as alienation.

Three varieties of alienation emerge as important in Marx's view. One of them may seem to be now less common, at least in America. The other two arguably persist to some degree, and Marx would have regarded them (in their twenty-first-century forms) as still a problem.

The one that has somewhat faded is this. In the mid-nineteenth century, there were numbers of privileged people who were essentially consumers (with money to spend), but who were hardly producers of anything. Conversely, there were huge numbers of producers—laboring in factories or as agricultural workers—who were only minimally consumers. The working class, whether urban or rural, simply had very little money to spend. From Marx's point of view, this was in both cases an unhealthy imbalance. Major consumers, whether or not they thought so, were missing something in life by not being productive. Productive workers who were only minimally consumers also had an unbalanced life.

It is worth saying a little about how these extremes have become modified. First, the reader may need to be convinced that there was a widespread phenomenon of wealthy people who simply did not work. One step toward grasping this is to read the novels of Jane Austen, written a half-century or so before Marx began to write but describing a world that had not greatly changed in that interval. Jane Austen's novels generally center on marriages, the coming together of a young woman and an eligible man. The eligible man will have money. Again and again in a Jane Austen novel, a young man moves into the area and immediately is known to be eligible, making so many thousand pounds a year. It is as if the man has a statement of his income attached to his back. Almost always this is income from investments or inheritance; he does not actually work.

People of this sort still exist. But my sense is that they are much less common. One reason for this may be a widespread sentiment that a mature adult ought to "do" something. Merely living off investments can be seen as mildly disreputable.

Similarly, while there still are very poor workers, who are only minimally consumers, this seems not quite as common as it was in Marx's day. This is partly a result of the rise of labor unions, which has led to at least some workers being better paid than would have been the case in the mid-nineteenth century. There also is the twenty-first-century phenomenon of the "consumer society," with its pervasive advertising and strong expectation that people in general will be acquiring "stuff." My guess is that Marx would have disliked almost everything about the consumer society. But he would have thought that the diminished imbalance between producing and consuming, at least, was a positive development.

Alienation connected with the kind of work one does, and the demands it makes on one, on the other hand, has not faded at all. On the contrary, it arguably has increased. Marx would regard this as increasingly against the needs (and the possibility of fulfillment) of human nature.

Alienation Connected with the Nature of Work

One kind of alienation in work, as Marx saw it, was intimately connected with exploitation. It should be noted that this is part of the relation (as Marx saw it) between two opposing groups, both of which had been developing in the century before Marx wrote. One group was the capitalists. The other group that grew as a direct result of capitalism was the proletariat (workers for wages). The first group, according to Marx, exploited the second.

In his *Capital,* Marx contended that the value of a product should be seen as the sum of the value of the raw materials plus the value of the labor that goes into making the product. In other words, the value of the labor is the final value minus the value of the raw materials, and Marx's clear implication is that the workers should be paid that much. They generally are not paid that much, however, because the capitalist takes profits. In Marx's view that is unjust.

Also Marx thought that the system alienates the workers from their work. An independent producer can think of the process and the product in personal terms, as "my thing," so to speak. The employed worker cannot have this. It all is someone else's thing.

Marx took this seriously. Nevertheless, it is not (from his point of view) the most important source of alienation involved in work. The major source, especially as presented in Marx's earlier writings, was the division of labor.[1] This had developed considerably in the preceding century. As the Industrial Revolution that began in the eighteenth century moved forward, it had become clear that there could be greater efficiency if some workers simply did the same thing over and over. The more repetitive the work of most people became, the more productive the system would become. The idea was that if people did the same thing constantly, they would be very likely to get good at it. There also would be no loss of time as they adjusted from one activity to another.

The extreme manifestation of this idea in the last hundred years is the factory assembly line in which each worker does one thing to what is being produced, before it is passed on to the next person. Marx lived before the assembly line was, so to speak, perfected. But the division of labor had already reached, in his day, a point at which many workers did one or two kinds of things over and over again.

The dullness of this kind of work is hard to estimate, although it is sometimes pointed out that it is consistent with interesting daydreams. All the same, even though such work is sometimes paid reasonably well, hardly anyone seems to enjoy it. From Marx's point of view, it is a major deformation of the structure of the human mind. To produce someone who is fully at home only in one work operation is, in Marx's view, like producing someone who is as much like a machine as like a person. Alternatively, one might view great skill at the one work operation, as opposed to limited skill at everything else, as rather like a person with a very large and muscular right arm and a withered and weak left arm.

The assembly line is the extreme example of specialization; but doctors, lawyers, and professors often specialize as well. Again, this may seem efficient. There might be a competitive advantage in spending almost all of one's work time on one narrow subject or activity. If you were about to undergo an operation on part X of your body, you would almost certainly prefer a physician who operated only on part X of the body.

Narrow specialization very often has advantages, not only for the specialist but also for those who desire the aid of someone with highly refined special skills. On the other hand, it can be seen as a deformation of the mind. Someone who could have a balanced and broad view of an area of knowledge instead has a much deeper view of a small part of the area and a somewhat sketchy view of the surrounding territory.

In some areas of knowledge, such as medicine, these disadvantages may seem rather small; my guess is that most readers would not think that they really represent a kind of "alienation." In the "human sciences" and the humanities, there could be a different response. Considerable specialization can undermine prospects for arriving at comprehensive views and also can make a subject less accessible to educated nonspecialists with lively minds.

Marx's primary focus, in any case, was more on the large number of ordinary workers than on doctors, lawyers, professors, and so on. The former group in his view were very often victims of the division of labor, even if they themselves might not have seen it that way. They also were condemned by the existing social structures to being "working class." We shortly will take up the kind of alienation that Marx thought was connected to consciousness of class divisions. The immediate point is that a "class system," of the sort that (in a very pronounced way) used to be dominant in Britain, throughout Europe, and in many other parts of the world, largely cut off members of different social classes from much meaningful contact with one another.[2]

Marx certainly was against such social polarization for a number of reasons. One was that it made it easier for the privileged classes not to be disturbed by what Marx saw as exploitation of workers. It also narrowed the range of experience and understanding, on both sides of the dividing line. Those who were privileged usually had very little sense of the experiences and sensibility of workers, and workers felt cut off from the privileged life of culture and of varied literary or intellectual interests.

Alienation in the Network of Personal Relations

Above all, while there were regular encounters between members of different social classes, few people really knew others of a different social class. It could be unusual to have an easy and meaningful conversation across the class divide. Very often someone's friends were of a similar social class.

It should be emphasized that all of this is a matter of degree and that people have varied widely in the conversations and the kinds of friends that they have had. All the same, there was (and to some extent still is) a pattern of frequent lack of connection. In an odd way, this tended to imprison people within the mental world of their own social class. They knew that there was something more "out there" but had relatively little sense of what it was like. Occasionally individuals (George Orwell was an example) crossed over and then back again. But for many workers the privileged classes, for whom they did jobs or saw regularly, were like the inhabitants of a foreign country. Awareness among the privileged class of the lives of workers was similarly limited.

Marx regarded this as a deformation of those on both sides of the class divide. His view was that economic circumstances—particularly those involved in the production of wealth—were at the root of this alienation. If the exploitation of workers could be ended and their earnings raised to a proper level, the psychological gap between the classes would be greatly diminished. If economic equality could be achieved, the psychological gap would be virtually eliminated.

In short, Marx's view was that the problem of alienation in personal relations (across class lines) required elimination of class lines and that this in turn required bringing the proletariat up to the standard of living of the other classes of society. At that point, distinct social classes would cease to exist, because the members of the social classes as they used to be would be on a par with each other.

The Marxist slogan "From each according to his ability; to each according to his need" captures the kind of equality that, in Marx's view, would end the kind of alienation just discussed. The map of the future that Marx provided is intended as a guide to this outcome. The first step is that workers of the world will unite and will revolt. They surely will succeed. (They have the greater numbers.) Then there will be, for a while, the dictatorship of the proletariat, in order to eliminate any attempts to reassert class privilege. This will be followed by a classless (and hence unified) society. Marxists (including Lenin) spoke of a final outcome in which the state (which had imposed its commands on a population that was not unified) would no longer be needed, once community self-management was possible. This was spoken of as the "withering away of the state."

This may seem to many readers like a fantasy world of the future. It certainly bears very little relation to actual developments in, say, the Soviet Union. In the Soviet Union (and other "communist" countries) the gap in well-being between the administrative or managerial classes on one hand, and ordinary workers on the other, was at a level comparable to that under capitalism. Part of what Marx meant by "communism" was a society of extreme equality. It should be clear that the so-called communist countries were far removed from this ideal and did not meet Marx's standards. If Marx had somehow traveled forward in time and arrived in the Soviet Union, he surely would have been sent to Siberia, or alternatively to a psychiatric clinic (a favorite Soviet repository for people who thought for themselves).

In conclusion, if we bear in mind that Marx's view of human nature is that its fulfillment requires the elimination of alienation, it is clear that he would be largely disappointed by what has happened since his lifetime. What he might regard as small advances have occurred here and there. The "class system" is less strong and less rigid in some countries than it had been. There have been experiments in developing factories in which work is not very specialized. No image, however, that is very like Marx's idea can be found in reality. Some of the ideals crop up in unexpected places. The French film À nous la liberté (1931) captures one element, depicting a future in which people would not be compelled to lead lives of entirely specialized work

Lives of entirely specialized work remain though, as do class systems and extreme contrasts between the rich and the poor. If the analysis that this chapter presents is right, the Scandinavian countries arguably are not as far from Marx's ideal as Soviet Russia and "communist" China have been. Clearly though, the ideal has never been achieved or even approximated. Whether it is practicable remains a question that is not at all easy to answer.

Notes

1. A very good study of Marx's early writings is contained in Robert C. Tucker, *Philosophy and Myth in Karl Marx* (Cambridge: Cambridge University Press, 1961).

2. Many readers will associate the class system with degrees of wealth. But, in living memory, it also involved in some places such things as accent or family name. In Britain, for example, there used to be a recognizable contrast between working class and privileged class accents.

Questions for Further Consideration

1. Why did Marx believe that much of the work that people do for a living is "alienated"?

2. Marx's view implies that someone who does not care at all for any other people is "alienated" and cannot have a satisfactory life. Is that true? Couldn't such a person, if lucky, have lots of fun?

Recommended Further Reading

Good introductions to the progression of Marx's thought are provided by Isaiah Berlin, *Karl Marx: His Life and Environment* (New York: Oxford University Press, 1959); and Robert Tucker, *Philosophy and Myth in Karl Marx* (Cambridge: Cambridge University Press, 1961).

Chapter 12

Sartre and Kierkegaard: Radical Incompleteness as the Human Lot

Jean-Paul Sartre's view of human nature to be discussed here is that we all are essentially free. This is central to his early book *Being and Nothingness*. It is mainly this book by which many philosophers know his work. In his later career Sartre was increasingly influenced by Marxism and moved toward a more complicated account of our lives. But we will be concentrating on *Being and Nothingness,* and to a considerable degree on the "nothingness" that is linked to inescapable freedom.

The idea of "nothingness" is key to a radical view of human nature as inescapably (for any individual) containing a multitude of possibilities. Because of this, human nature (according to Sartre) is persistently to have choices. Even if we strongly dislike this and would like simply to remain what we are, it turns out, in Sartre's view, that what we are propels us from one choice to the next.

Sartre's Affinity to Kierkegaard

The "nothingness" on which Sartre dwelt is not an emptiness or vacuity. It is rather an incompleteness or lack of definiteness that all humans share and that Sartre thought cannot be attributed to objects. It can be seen as a personal problem for all of us, because it leaves open all of the decisions that we have to make. We are "condemned to be free." A somewhat similar incompleteness is a major tenet of a book by Søren Kierkegaard, written nearly a century before.

Sartre and Kierkegaard might seem to be an odd couple. Sartre is best known as a French mid-twentieth-century exponent of what he publicized as existentialism. He had no use for religion, held radical views on a variety of subjects, and flirted with Marxism. Kierkegaard lived in Denmark a century before Sartre, was a dedicated Lutheran, and devoted himself largely to examination of the relation between religious faith and human psychology. These two clearly had opposite attitudes on religion and many social issues. But Kierkegaard anticipated much of a view of what was distinctive in human life that was Sartre's most dramatic philosophical contribution.

Kierkegaard's view emerged in one of the two major works that examined the psychological role in human life of religious faith. These are *Fear and Trembling* and *Sickness unto Death*. *Fear and Trembling* centers on the Old Testament story of Abraham and Isaac, especially on Abraham's decision to obey God's command to sacrifice his son Isaac. As any reader of the Bible knows, Isaac was not sacrificed, because at the last minute Abraham was told to sacrifice instead a ram that was caught in the thicket.

This story can be seen in a number of ways. It was common among some of the very ancient inhabitants of the Middle East to sacrifice the eldest child to the gods. What happened to Abraham and Isaac (and to the ram) could be taken as a "just so" story, marking a transition among the ancient ancestors of the Hebrews from human sacrifice to animal sacrifice. (There is a later transition, marked in the Old Testament, to a policy of no sacrifice at all.) The more usual reading, though, is that the story represents a test of faith.

Kierkegaard had no quarrel with this interpretation, but he took pains to point out the extreme nature of the test. Read about in Sunday school, it sounds like a nice but odd story. Its niceness has a lot to do with the happy ending. However, if we move slowly through the story and put ourselves into the mental state of a man who thinks that God really expects him to sacrifice his son, Kierkegaard contended that we should feel deeply disturbed. What is asked could well be seen as wrong and irrational. But it also becomes an expression of religious faith. Kierkegaard took this to support his view that genuine religious faith is deeper and more difficult than it is merely to say yes to a bunch of propositions.

Kierkegaard contended that Abraham's willingness to sacrifice his son was counterintuitive and countermoral (but still, in his view, right). In these respects it is an example of extreme religious faith—so extreme that very few people who think of themselves as religious could stomach it. Kierkegaard regarded this as very positive. The more "irrational" the choice, the deeper the faith can be.[1]

Sickness unto Death is the book that points forward to Sartre's view. A major topic in it is despair. The book claims that it is to some degree an affliction of almost everyone. Kierkegaard argued that despair can be like a low grade illness, something that is unpleasant and detracts from life but that people usually will be hardly aware of. Occasionally it may flare up into something quite noticeable.

The root of the despair is this: to be a finite human being is to be unanchored or incomplete. The only remedy is a firm connection with God, namely entire religious faith. This completes or anchors what we are.

Sartre's analysis in *Being and Nothingness* of human nature in effect accepts a description a little like Kierkegaard's of the illness, while rejecting Kierkegaard's cure. "Nothingness" is a term for a radical incompleteness in the nature of any human being at any point in her or his life. This incompleteness allows for a wide range of possibilities and hence amounts to freedom.

The word *freedom* normally has positive associations. This is especially the case because *freedom* often connotes an absence of burdens (including servitude) or of unwelcome impositions. When Sartre spoke of freedom, though, he meant a general landscape of open possibilities, more of them than we could manage to contemplate. He assessed this extreme openness of possibilities as in some ways disconcerting and uncomfortable. Perhaps this falls short of despair, but Sartre regarded it as definitely not pleasant.

This way of thought may seem more persuasive if one attends to the many examples Sartre gave of what amount to failed attempts to escape from freedom. Some of these examples are linked to the charm of being a definite kind of person with, as it were, a firm nature.

We generally would like this, Sartre thought. This can be part of the appeal of having a definite role with which one can merge. For example, Bloggs can imagine a world in which people say, "You can count on Bloggs. He always will . . ." It can help if Bloggs has very definite responsibilities to fulfill. It might be even better if Bloggs wore a uniform of some sort.

Perhaps Bloggs will in general stay within this role, with which he will be most comfortable. But at odd and surprising moments there could be an unexpected departure. People who have been thrown off balance often are like that. Sartre would see it as an instance of something revealing itself that is a deep feature of Bloggs' humanity.

Freedom and Predictability

The account thus far of Sartre's view of human nature is stark and straightforward. Because each of us has an inner "nothingness," it will be impossible to predict our behavior with 100 percent certainty. Our choices are not entirely predetermined.

Indeed, according to Sartre, we have the uneasy sense that we are not able to predict our own behavior with complete certainty. In that respect, we always have choices. Part of the uneasiness of freedom is that, on the whole, we might not like our own possible choices.

Sartre suggested something like this as explaining a widespread phenomenon—fear of heights. Some might think that this—involving an anxiety when high up, even if the balcony or other support we are on is clearly solid and safe—is a neurotic phobia. Sartre saw it as at root a fear that we might suddenly (impulsively) throw ourselves from what we are standing on.

Quite possibly there are some suicides that do have this impulsive character and have no connection at all with anything like a considered preference. This might be one of the reasons why people who have been prevented from committing suicide are so often grateful. Be that as it may, the fear of doing something one does not want to do is a striking manifestation of a looseness in the sources of our behavior. We cannot predict with entire confidence what might take over at the crucial moment.

The reader may have noticed the phrases "100 percent certainty" or "complete certainty," and the words *entire* and *entirely,* in this account of Sartre's assessment of the ability to predict our behavior. This might serve as a red flag, alerting one to the fact that Sartre's philosophy (like most philosophy worth taking seriously) is more complicated than it appears at first. Within each of us, Sartre said, there is a nothingness. But there also can be (in his view) structures of behavior and preference which are such that our choices can have a degree of predictability. Often we are *virtually* certain about what we will choose or what someone we know well will choose.

In short, if the question is whether we or other people can predict our behavior, Sartre's answer would be "often, yes." If the question is whether we or other people can predict our behavior with entire certainty, the answer becomes no.

An extended discussion of this in *Being and Nothingness* centers on a situation in which Sartre, fatigued during a hike with friends, chooses to rest.[2] It is clear during Sartre's examination of this imagined case that his stopping to rest would not surprise anyone who knows Sartre well. It might be tempting to take the view that, if fatigue caused Sartre to stop, then what happened is simply part of the causal order. How, one might wonder, does "freedom" play a part in the event?

We shortly will take up Sartre's long discussion of this case. It does provide what amounts to an answer. But it may help the reader in grasping the answer if we first look briefly at recent Anglo-American lines of thought about causes and effects.

One point to be emphasized is that a great many things happen as they do because of a number of causal factors. Something may burst into flame because someone lit a match next to it and also because it had not been treated with flame retardant. If car X hits car Y, this is because car Y was driving rather slowly in front of it and also because the driver of X was using a cell phone and not steadily looking at the road. It has sometimes been suggested that when an unfortunate event has many causes, our search for *the* cause can be really an inquiry into who or what was most at fault.[3]

Let us follow this a little further. If it is true that event P caused event Q, the reader might suppose that this implies that whenever P occurs Q will then happen. This would be a mistake. Suppose that P is some extremely risky behavior on someone's part, such as driving at high speed on streets on which children often play. This can lead to a terrible accident, and no one would hesitate to say that the hazardous driving was the cause of the accident. But this can be true even if the same driver had driven in exactly the same way on other occasions and no harm had ensued.

We now can return to Sartre, as he rests from the exertion of his hike. The immediate cause of his stopping was fatigue. But, as he points out, some of his companions are fatigued also but do not stop. They may like being fatigued. Part of the appeal of some athletic activities, including long distance running, indeed can be the sense of having thoroughly used one's body and having gone to the limit in this.

So, in Sartre's account, there are at least two causes (not merely one) of his stopping to rest. One is fatigue and another one is that he does not enjoy being fatigued. Many things, however, will be connected with Sartre's unwillingness to heighten his fatigue. At the most basic level, he points out, an attitude toward one's own body is crucial.

Again, in appreciating the line of analysis, one must take care not to think too simply. The simple response might be to think that there are two types of attitude toward the body. Some people (including those who do not stop to rest) are positive about their bodies, and Sartre clearly was not. To treat things as this simple would be to ignore some facts. Some people are positive about their bodies, treating them to long baths in warm water, various lotions, and so on, but not long sweaty hikes. Sartre may have been inclined, as we sometimes say, not to be a very "physical" person in the context of a long sweaty hike but may have had different attitudes in other contexts.

Further, Sartre made it clear that even though he was fatigued and had a history of not liking fatigue, this did not guarantee that he would stop to rest. There are two imaginable ways in which he could have responded differently.

One, which he mentioned, is that he could have at that moment made what might be called an "existential choice." This would be one that involved the kind of person he was and the general way in which he behaved. He could have decided (as he was about to rest) to become more athletic and not to let fatigue bother him.

There is another alternative that Sartre did not mention. He could have, on impulse, decided not to rest, with the thought that (perhaps just this once) he would act as if he was athletic and did not mind fatigue. Almost all of us at some moments will act out of character, on impulse doing something that we would not normally do. Very often this may be thought of (and may turn out to be) a "one-off" kind of behavior.

Be that as it may, Sartre in this case stayed in character. Anyone who knew Sartre at all well could have predicted this, he observed. Bear in mind that this is distinct from any claim that his resting could have been predicted with entire certainty. Sartre would certainly reject such a strong claim. His stopping to rest was, so to speak, in the cards. But it was not a sure thing.

This all points toward a more complex image of human nature than what we began with. Nothingness remains a distinctive and important feature of human nature. But structures of characteristic behavior also become part of the picture.

It may not be entirely clear whether structures of characteristic behavior are part of everyone's life. Perhaps there are some people so dominated by a wide variety of impulses, or by capriciousness, that their behavior is not even moderately predictable? Most of us however are at least somewhat like Sartre (in his self-description). Our friends and colleagues on many occasions have a good idea of what we will choose.

One might think of this as sketchy decision patterns in the midst of nothingness. This somewhat qualifies our nothingness. But also we might take another look at the choice of wording that *nothingness* represents. There are varieties of late Buddhist philosophy, some of which feed into Zen Buddhism, that emphasize *sunyata* (or *shunyata*) as our actual or possible inner nature. The usual translation of *sunyata* is as "emptiness." Reliable scholars though have told me that it could equally be translated as "openness." Similarly, what Sartre spoke of as "nothingness" could equally be rendered as "openness." Clearly the openness (if one is willing to use the word) is not the same in the two cases. In Zen Buddhism, openness is in some respects an achievement, representing a sort of creative improvisation. In Sartre's account an openness of choice is the essence of humanity.

The Project of Constructing and Modifying a Self

When Sartre conceded that his friends could easily have predicted that he would stop to rest, he also suggested that the choice on this occasion rests on a more fundamental choice of a kind of life. The suggestion is that human beings (often? always?) have fundamental projects that involve being a certain kind of person leading a certain kind of life. Sartre's interest in fundamental projects led him to biographical examinations of the lives of the playwright Jean Genet and the poet Baudelaire.

If all or many of us have fundamental projects in life, it is tempting to suppose that these begin to take shape in childhood. Indeed it is often suggested that what so-and-so is like has a great deal to do with her or his relations with parents and siblings in the early years of childhood. But hardly anyone would contend that the fundamental project will have assumed its final form, or anything very close to it, by the time we are teenagers. As Sartre insisted, we continue to make choices. Sartre praised Genet for his intelligent modification, as an adult, of his fundamental project. If this is possible, then smaller modifications throughout our life are surely possible.

This connects with an element in David Hume's philosophy that was not discussed in Chapter 9. Hume's ethical writings pay considerable attention to the factors that determine how we evaluate people's characters and their virtues. An obvious related thought is that some of us might decide, in part because of how others react to us, to change somewhat the kind of person we are. Hume took this seriously, and asked in at least two places how such a change of self is possible and also what the difficulties are in making such a change. In the *Treatise of Human Nature*, he suggested that such a transformation may turn out to be virtually impossible. In his essay "The Sceptic," he suggested that if there is a change, it will not be direct and immediate. If it takes place at all, it will be a gradual process, relying on changes in a person's "bent" and habits.[4] Sartre might agree with Hume on much of this; it is hard to be sure.

Nothingness and Determinism

Freedom is often thought of as opposite to determinism. It is therefore not surprising that Sartre rejected determinism, especially the psychological determinism of Freud. All the same, the philosophical picture is more complicated than one might think. We can get at this by examining what the thesis of determinism amounts to and why many philosophers find it irresistible.

Determinism is the claim that, when someone is making a choice, anyone who knows all relevant facts and all the laws of nature will be able to predict with entire certainty what that person will choose. If X does Y, a determinist will insist that Y "was in the cards all along." If freedom means that X had more than one genuine possibility, then determinism implies that X is not free.

Here is a line of thought that has led many philosophers to accept determinism. A pivotal claim is that—generally speaking—if anything occurs or exists, there must be a cause of this. The phrase "generally speaking" is intended to allow for what many philosophers have considered the one imaginable exception: the existence of God, which is widely held to have no cause (unless one stipulates that the existence of God is a unique case of self-caused existence).

If every event has a cause, a further step on this path to determinism is to assume that causes necessitate their effects. If X causes Y, then Y not merely will occur or exist, its occurrence or existence will have been 100 percent certain (given the causal power of X). This, it has been contended, is true even for the way in which psychological causes necessitate our thought and behavior.

If every choice we think we make is necessitated by a cause, then it can be argued that freedom is an illusion. Many philosophers, however, who have accepted determinism have maintained nevertheless that we have some freedom. This view (called "soft determinism") holds that "freedom" can be interpreted to be compatible with determinism. One thought is that to be free is to be able to do what you want to do (whether or not what you want to do has been causally determined). Even if what you want, besides being itself determined, determines what you do, you still would pass this test for being "free."

Sartre had no use for moves of this sort. Neither did he accept the view that causes necessitate their effects. The proposition that causes necessitate effects does have considerable appeal, especially to those who prefer reality to be orderly. But it can be argued that we sometimes judge X to be the cause of Y when X makes Y much more probable than it otherwise would have been, even if the high probability ascribed to Y is less than 100 percent. If this is accepted, the case for determinism is seriously undermined.

Some philosophers have argued that the denial of determinism entails randomness of behavior. This line of thought, along with Sartre's insistence that human life involves continuous choosing (and that the choices are never 100 percent predictable), may suggest that Sartre's image of normal human life is, if not quite random, still somewhat chaotic. This would be mistaken however.

It should again be emphasized that Sartre's discussion of cases such as that of his stopping to rest on the hike points toward an image of human life as normally quite structured, and indeed as largely unified around chosen projects in life. This applies even to small bits of activity within everyday life. "A gesture," Sartre said, "refers to a weltanschauung [i.e., a worldview] and we sense it" (p. 589). A highly integrated life emerges, in Sartre's view as the norm, and a chaotic life would be the exception.

Even if we have made fundamental choices that structure the projects of our life, this does not guarantee that we have a clear understanding of what we have chosen. Someone for example who persistently "screws up" in life, thwarting her or his own plans, almost certainly has not thoughtfully arrived at the project of making her or his life a mess. Indeed such a person might benefit from understanding what the fundamental choices have been. This would improve the chances of being able intelligently to make different kinds of choices that lead to a more fulfilling kind of life.

Existentialist philosophy such as Sartre's led to a distinctive kind of psychoanalysis: existential psychoanalysis. This was designed to give a clearer view of what one's choices actually amounted to (as distinct from what one said to oneself about what they were). Sartre rejected Freud's thesis that there is a realm of the "unconscious" that plays a huge role in human life. Rather Sartre's position can be described as holding that there is a territory of the unaware, of choices and motivations that hide in plain sight. If we can become more aware of what we actually have been choosing, we can achieve more command over ourselves.

Existential psychoanalysis in short is a therapy of greater self-understanding. What is to be understood is a somewhat unified structure of choices. The principle, Sartre said, "is that man is a totality and not a collection" (p. 728). Once the choices that underlie the totality are understood and appreciated, we can have a greater power to re-choose.

The contrast between existential psychoanalysis and the "empirical" psychoanalysis of Freud or of Alfred Adler then turns out to be sharp. "Empirical psychoanalysis seeks to determine the complex" (as in, say, the Oedipus complex), "the very name of which indicates the polyvalence of all the impulses and meanings that are referred back to it. "Polyvalence" points toward the variety of ways in which things a disturbance or a motivation can be manifested. Existentialist psychoanalysis in contrast, Sartre said, "seeks to determine the original choice" (p. 728).

As Sartre saw it, "empirical" psychoanalysis then focuses on causes, which can include experiences in early childhood and also various drives, such as the libido that Freud often focuses on, and the will to power (which has a similar central role for Adler). Freud's psychoanalysis is deterministic: despite appearances, there turn out to be no accidents or slips of the tongue. All is determined by hidden causes. In contrast, existentialist psychoanalysis focuses on contingency: the contingency of what we choose, including the original choice of a fundamental project in life. The environment can act on the subject, Sartre insisted, "only to the exact extent that he comprehends it; that is, transforms it into a situation" (p. 731). Hence the "objective" descriptions of deterministic psychologies do not help us. We must concentrate instead on how a person construes and (through choices) constructs her or his world.

Notes

1. Many pious people thought that Kierkegaard went too far, and there was a small riot at his funeral.

2. See *Being and Nothingness,* trans. Hazel Barnes (New York: Washington Square Press, 1966), p. 584ff. Further references to *Being and Nothingness* will be parenthetical in the text, and will be to this edition.

3. Cf. H. L. A. Hart and Tony Honoré, *Causation in the Law* (Oxford: Clarendon Press, 1981).

4. See *Treatise of Human Nature*, 2nd ed., ed. L. A. Selby-Bigge, rev. P. H. Nidditch (Oxford: Clarendon Press, 1978), p. 608; and also "The Sceptic" (1742) in *Essays*, ed. Eugene F. Miller (Indianapolis: Liberty Classics, 1985), pp. 169–171.

Questions for Further Consideration

1. Why is it that Sartre believed that we are "condemned to be free"?

2. How did Kierkegaard associate the phenomena that this involves with a crisis of religious faith?

3. Is the indeterminacy of self that Sartre analyzed necessarily a bad thing?

Recommended Further Reading

A variety of perspectives on Sartre is provided by Paul Arthur Schilpp, ed., in *The Philosophy of Jean-Paul Sartre* (La Salle, IL: Open Court, 1981). Karen L. Carr and Philip J. Ivanhoe bring together Kierkegaard and a great Chinese Daoist in an interesting way in *The Sense of Antirationalism: The Religious Thought of Zhuangzi and Kierkegaard* (New York: Seven Bridges Press, 2000).

Chapter 13

Arendt: Making Oneself Distinct

It seems unlikely that Hannah Arendt would have regarded her *The Human Condition* as contributing to a theory of human nature. She spoke of the problem of human nature as "unanswerable." To formulate an essence for ourselves "would be like jumping over our own shadows."[1]

The crucial insight is that distinctness is a central feature of human life.[2] She carefully analyzed human distinctness as going beyond otherness or separateness. Two people imaginably could be separate but also entirely or almost entirely alike. Distinctness requires that we are not entirely or almost entirely the same as others in our natures.

Our life, according to Arendt, is an ongoing process of projecting a distinct image of ourselves, mainly through our actions and our speech. It is important to bear in mind that this often is not self-conscious and deliberate. People sometimes self-consciously do and say things in order to project an image of themselves. In many such cases the image they intend is deceptive or is designed to make them seem better than they are. Much of the time though what we say or do is not self-consciously intended to project a certain image.[3] Rather it simply "gives us away," revealing something of what we are like, even though the revelation could not be further from our thoughts.

It further should be emphasized, as Arendt said very well, that the manifestation of who we are is often unclear or ambiguous (p. 162). It comes to pass, as she said, "in the same manner

169

as the notoriously unreliable manifestations of ancient oracles, which, according to Heraclitus, 'neither reveal nor hide in words, but give manifest signs.'" This is related to "the impossibility, as it were, to solidify in words the living essence of the person as it shows itself in the flux of action and speech . . ." (p. 161).

Need there be for every person a projection of a distinct self? If so (or approximately so), does Hannah Arendt's account of this amount to a theory of human nature, or at least an element of a theory? These are questions we must address before we take up the implications for human life of what Arendt said.

Distinctness and Human Nature

A first question is whether distinctness is prior to any expression or revelation of it in speech or action. This is more likely to occur to a reader today than it would have to Arendt, because of the widening awareness that even at birth everyone has distinct DNA. So in some sense distinctness is there from the start.

Clearly, however, the nature that we reveal in speech and action goes well beyond such inherited characteristics. DNA may well play a role in shaping personality. But it is far from clear that it always, or even usually, has a decisive role. Our upbringing and the circumstances of our childhood can make enormous differences in the personality that we develop. It is hard to deny, at the extremes, that being surrounded by love, or being treated brutally, will make a difference.

Is Arendt concerned with distinctness in the sense of differentiation from other people? A sympathetic reading suggests that what she had in mind is not merely differentiation but rather what we might call "distinctness as a person," which would certainly include personality. Whatever the causal factors are in what someone becomes, it is only when someone can be witnessed as a person that we can have a sense of the distinctness with which Arendt is concerned. To "know" somebody, or to have a sense of what that person is like, requires contact with the person or at least some representations of what such contact would reveal.

If it is generally true of human beings that their distinctness (the distinctness with which Arendt is concerned) is expressed in actions and speech, how can Arendt have denied that she had a theory of human nature? Here is one possible answer: what Arendt had in mind as a view of human nature involves an "essence," which presumably would hold for all (or perhaps almost all?) humans. For us to meet this standard for a shared human nature, we all, or almost all, would have to be like each other. Arendt plainly thought that this is not the case.

Do all humans (past a certain age) project a distinct nature? Arguably not: those who are catatonic do not, unless of course one counts being catatonic as a nature. Even if those who are catatonic are held not to project a distinct nature though, it would still be the case that almost all humans (past a certain age) project a distinct nature. So why did Arendt think that she had nothing to say on the topic of human nature?

An interpretation of the word *essence* (p. 12) seems to me crucial in this. "Essence" can be taken broadly or narrowly. A broad construction (of an idea of the essence of humanity) is that to have an essence is to have a nature that is shared with all, or almost all, humans. A narrow construction is that something can count as *in* the essence of humanity if it is part of the nature of all, or almost all, human beings, even though other parts or aspects of the nature of human beings can vary widely.

The suspicion is that Arendt was using "essence" in a broad sense. If theories of human nature require this broad sense, then clearly she was right in denying that she had a theory of human nature. We are not all, or almost all, very much alike. Given this, she also would be right in suggesting that there is something absurd in the idea of a human nature.

The reader though will know that none of the theories discussed thus far has posited such a broad uniformity. When Aristotle characterized man as a rational animal and Hobbes spoke of the appetitive and competitive nature of humanity, neither was claiming that everybody (or almost everybody) is alike in a broad range of characteristics. The claim is rather that humans (different from one another as they may be) by and large have a degree of rationality (Aristotle) or tend to be appetitive and competitive (Hobbes).

Given this narrow and limited scope that theories of human nature generally have, we might well conclude that Arendt (by traditional standards) did have a theory of human nature: namely, that it generally included a tendency to express distinctness in speech and action. Not only is this as much a theory of human nature as anything that Aristotle or Hobbes held, but also it is itself a distinctive theory. There are hints of something like it in Sartre's philosophy, but Arendt's fully developed view is unique.

The Development of Distinctness

Even babies can have elements of distinctive personality. Some cry a lot, for various reasons; some are relatively serene. With increasing control of the body, some babies show themselves eager to explore and others are more passive. Not all of these elements of personality, of course, necessarily correlate with personality in later life.

The broad outlines of what there is in early years of life are sometimes referred to as temperament. In the early modern period in Europe, the four types of temperament were thought to be sanguine, melancholic, choleric, and phlegmatic. Your temperament would have represented at least a starting point in the person you are. Probably for most of us it is more than a starting point; rather, it represents a very broad outline of the kind of person we continue to be. Within the broad outline, of course, it is almost inevitable that there will be some changes.

What we are like when we come to have some degree of real control over our lives is generally spoken of as character. The words *character* and *personality* are not far apart in their meanings. They both are intended to capture what we are like. However, each contains a special emphasis on some elements of what we are like. A description of someone's personality is likely to dwell on how he or she reacts to various kinds of people and situations, placing great emphasis on the style of personal interactions. Personalities are often described as charming, outgoing, reclusive, shy, serene, or disturbed.

A description of a character, in contrast, will place great emphasis on tendencies toward morally virtuous or unworthy behavior and also on the ability to cope with difficulties or setbacks. Experiences of great disappointment or of losing something that seemed important are often spoken of as tests of character and sometimes also are said to build character. Character thus is thought of as connected with strength, perseverance, and reliability. Someone who is very good at resisting temptation and at avoiding irrational behavior might be spoken of as having a strong character. Someone, on the other hand, who is easily swayed and is not good at resisting temptation could be spoken of as "lacking character."[4]

The revealing of distinctness, whether what is revealed falls mainly under the head of personality or of character, is an activity that has many dimensions. It can reflect not only elements of what we are like, but also how we feel about ourselves. This self-directed attitude can be quite positive, evident especially when the revelation has a proud tone, quite negative (as when revealing oneself includes expressions of guilt or shame), or wry (when we clearly are not proud of our foibles or little failures, but can live with them). Self-consciously revealing oneself also can play a role in the development of self.[5] It can serve the functions, that is, of consciously assessing what can be improved or alternatively can be endorsed. The person who consciously reveals himself or herself may then, if the self-directed attitude is mainly positive, stabilize and enlarge tendencies.

What Arendt's Account May Teach Us about the Limits of Theories of Human Nature

The final remarks in this chapter will form a bridge to the conclusions of the next and final chapters. Theories of human nature play many roles. One of them is to explore what we all, or almost all, have (at least to some degree) in common. People often speak of our common humanity. Theories of human nature tend to reinforce the view that there is such a thing.

How much sense there is in the idea of a common humanity will be explored in the final chapter. Let us assume, at least for the present, that it makes some sense. Hannah Arendt's work helps us to see that, even so, it represents one side of a picture in which there are two sides.

The two sides can be summed up as follows. One side involves an ability to identify with features of other people's lives. The other side involves awareness of features that are not so easy to identify with, and indeed may seem strange.

There are areas of life in which we can compare other people to ourselves and see that there are tendencies in their behavior that we can discern (to some degree, and in some form) in our own. What these areas are of course continues to be open to debate. Arguably they may include parts of life that normally are governed by (and that exhibit) rationality, as Aristotle would insist. They may include also (as Hobbes would insist) areas in which people often are "looking out for number one" and comparing what they get or achieve to what others get or achieve.

Some areas of life involve things that would be experienced as highly negative by almost anyone. One example is that of parents who lose a child. Other examples include people who have been tortured for some period of time, or who have sunk into lives of thorough misery. Much as almost anyone can immediately sympathize with parents who have lost a child, we also can identify with the torture victim or the thoroughly miserable person (especially if the misery seems to be the product of circumstances, and unavoidable under those circumstances). Almost all of us may think that, given those conditions, we might well have very similar experiences.

The second side of our relation to other people's natures and experiences is the one brought out so well by Hannah Arendt. Much in life centers on our views of uncommon human natures, ways in which other people exhibit qualities or have experiences that we cannot easily relate to. Alongside our experiences of what seems like a common humanity, we have views of behavior or experiences that startle, fascinate, disturb, or mystify us. In the end we may have a sense that everyone, or almost everyone, we encounter or might encounter is at least somewhat different—and distinct in personality—from us. This element of unfamiliarity and unpredictability can make some moments difficult. Overall, it makes the life experience much more fascinating than it would have been if we were all very much alike.

Notes

1. *The Human Condition* (Garden City, NY: Doubleday Anchor Books, 1959), p. 12. All subsequent quotes of Arendt are from this edition.

2. Ibid., pp. 155ff.

3. Neither is it always (or even usually) the case that what is primarily intended by the doer (of an action) is the disclosure of his or her own image—contrary to the quote from Dante at the top of p. 155, *The Human Condition*—at least if by "intended" is meant "consciously intended."

4. For a much fuller discussion, see my *Character* (New York: Oxford University Press, 1991).

5. John Kekes has suggested that this is a major feature of the work of the great French essayist Michel de Montaigne. See *The Enlargement of Life* (Ithaca: Cornell University Press, 2006).

Questions for Further Consideration

1. Does everyone project a distinct image? Aren't there people who are nondescript, whose image is always fuzzy and makes it seem that they are not really there?

2. Is distinctness generally an advantage or a disadvantage in life? Isn't it sometimes a plus not to be noticed?

Recommended Further Reading

Two good books on Hannah Arendt are Elizabeth Young-Bruehl, *Hannah Arendt: For Love of the World* (New Haven: Yale University Press, 2004); and Seyla Ben-Habib, *The Reluctant Modernism of Hannah Arendt* (Thousand Oaks, CA: Sage, 1996).

Chapter 14

Some Additional Views in Brief: Ibn al-Arabi, Spinoza, Pascal, and Rousseau

The four philosophers discussed in this chapter are not known principally for their views of human nature. For the most part, these views did not play a central role in their philosophies. Nevertheless each of them said interesting things that imply something about human nature. What they said may not amount to "theories" of human nature, but at the least they claim to tell us something important about it. These putative insights contribute to a kaleidoscope of views of human nature. But they can be presented more briefly than the other views that have been discussed.

The thirteenth-century philosopher Ibn al-Arabi was born in southern Spain when it was still under Islamic control, but most of his career was spent in the eastern Mediterranean region. His major book, *The Bezels of Wisdom,* was written in Damascus.[1]

Baruch Spinoza was a Jewish philosopher who lived in the Netherlands in the seventeenth century. He was excommunicated by his synagogue because of his unusual views.

Ibn al-Arabi and Spinoza shared the unusual idea that our identity is closely linked to God. This was a heresy, or at least verged on one, in the major forms of Judaism, Christianity, and Islam. In all of these religions, a drastic separation between a human being and God was taken for granted. We could be in touch with God, so to speak, through prayer or a personal revelation, but the being that we are in touch with will have a totally different kind of reality from ours. God created a universe—definitely separate from God the creator—of which we are a part.

Even though Ibn al-Arabi and Spinoza both held that our identity is closely linked to God, the details and also the contexts of their views differ significantly.

The view that *The Bezels of Wisdom* develops is in one respect typical of Muslim texts, going back to the sacred Koran (which is regarded as God's revelation via the angel Gabriel to the prophet Mohammad). It is made clear in the Koran that both the Old and New Testaments in the Bible are holy books, and that such figures as Moses, Elijah, and Jesus are prophets of God. Much of the discussion in *The Bezels of Wisdom* focuses on great prophets who had been described in the Bible. Ibn al-Arabi's emphasis is on strategies of personal fulfillment and of salvation.

His stance in discussing such strategies is that of a particular kind of Muslim. He was a Sufi. Sufism is a form of Islam that (unlike most other forms) is preoccupied with the mystical nature of our awareness of God. In some sense, in the Sufi view, each of us has a oneness with God. We are like dispersed parts of God's mind. This can be understood and expressed in various ways.

The simplest expression is to say "I am one with God." This sounds rather like the central claim of the *Upanishads* (cf. Chapter 3). It also constitutes a heresy from the point of view of the major forms of Islam, as it also does in virtually any form of Christianity or Judaism. A Sufi who said "I am God" was executed for this in Baghdad in the tenth century CE.

Ibn al-Arabi's position was not so simple or direct. He did, however, believe that there is something in our nature that links us to God. We can have an intimate awareness of God, and this can be an important and valuable part of our lives. This implies that it is human nature to have this capability, and to be such that great fulfillment requires an intimate connection with God. If you happen to agree with Ibn al-Arabi (and some Jews and Christians, along of course with Sufis, would agree), you would think that this is an important insight into an element of human nature.

This Sufi view lent itself to an ecstatic religious sensibility. Bear in mind that the etymology of *ecstatic* involves standing out from oneself: in effect, getting out of oneself. We get out of our finite human selves by realizing our connection with God. This could involve poetry, music, and dance (such as that of whirling dervishes). It should be emphasized that ecstatic religious experiences are definitely not limited to Sufis. One might think of the mystical experiences of St. Teresa of Avila and various other Christian and Jewish examples.

Spinoza also held a view that verged on a claim of oneness with God. In it there is a clearer sense of an identity, of anyone or anything with God than there is in Ibn al-Arabi's position. The central claim is that there is only one substance in the world, namely God. We may think of ourselves as independent substances, but really we are not. There are no substances independent of God.

Often a philosophy will center on a bold claim, which turns out to be surrounded by qualifications. In the *Upanishads* it is alleged that we are one with Brahman, but that does not mean that you are (or I am) everything or that we are perfect. It does mean that there is an important element of each of us that is in some sense pure being, but this turns out to be compatible with the fact that many of the actions and thoughts (in the layers of self that are most manifest in everyday life) may be far from pure.

Spinoza's view is that each of us is a mode of the one truly real substance (God). Spinoza defined a substance as "that which is in itself and is conceived through itself." Only God meets this criterion. We, Spinoza thought, have to be conceived in terms of our relation to God. By "mode" he meant a modification, "or that which is in another thing through which also it is conceived." God, who in Spinoza's view is the entire universe, is what we are in and through which we may be conceived.

This existence as a mode of God definitely does not mean that any of us is godlike or perfect. You might think of yourself as, in Spinoza's view, a "differentiated manifestation." Each manifestation of the real substance of God is different from the others, and none is perfect.

Could this be viewed as a claim about human nature? The claim of an inner connection with God (a substance of which each of us is a mode) seems to say something about human nature. Perhaps what it says can be put in experiential terms as follows. Anyone will experience her or his life as a succession of experiences, thoughts, emotions, and actions. These will be constantly changing, and all of these sequences also will have individual qualities: your succession of experiences, and so on, will not be quite like anyone else's. All the same, each of us has the strong sense that we remain the same person through all of the changes. There is some underlying truth here of what we are that holds for everybody.

You know that you are the same person as you were ten years ago, but that person may well have been very different from you. If there is a *you* that persists through time, remaining the same person, it cannot be thought of in terms of constant features of your experience, because the features keep changing. There has to be an underlying (and in some respects unchanging) impersonal you. One could view this as the *atman* of the *Upanishads,* or (as Spinoza implied) as your nature as a mode of God.

This is an unusual point of view, but Spinoza made it impressive. It would be hard to regard Spinoza's writing as focusing mainly on human nature. But it does offer what many readers might regard as insights. The view of our relation to God would go at the top of any list. Spinoza did say some other things about human nature, but these are much closer to ordinary common sense. Human beings, he pointed out, have a basic desire for what is thought beneficial to oneself. The main requirement for having a free, fulfilled life then is to have figured out what is genuinely beneficial for you.

Blaise Pascal was French, and like Spinoza lived in the seventeenth century. He was very different from Spinoza in a number of respects. Like most of the population of France he was Roman Catholic. Also (linked to his Catholicism) he regarded our individual natures as representing a thoroughly basic truth about us. There is nothing in Pascal's views that verges on heresy. Pascal in fact was (besides being a great mathematician) a deeply religious man. But his religious beliefs centered on the problems that we finite and flawed beings have in satisfying the requirements of an entirely separate supreme being (i.e., God).

He had some sympathy for Jansenism. Jansenism was roughly to Roman Catholicism what Puritanism was to Protestant Christianity. It demanded more seriousness and self-control than most forms of the religion did.

Pascal's most widely known line of thought indeed focused on strategy for achieving salvation. It was generally assumed that only someone who had had the correct religious allegiance could enter heaven. As Pascal took this, it meant that you would have to believe in the truth of Christianity in order to reach heaven. Some people in the seventeenth century were beginning to have doubts about the truth of revealed Christianity. There had been many attempts to prove the existence of God on the part of philosophers like St. Anselm, St. Thomas Aquinas, and Descartes, but Pascal clearly thought that these proofs were not effective in ending all doubt. How could he persuade doubters to become good Christians?

The answer was what became known as Pascal's wager. It starts from the presumption that everyone would like to go to heaven, instead of the alternatives (hell, purgatory, or limbo—the latter being a quiet place in the suburbs of hell, reserved for virtuous people who did not have the correct religious faith). Suppose that you simply think that you don't know whether God exists or not. Pascal then appeals to your self-interest.

If you (as it were) bet on God's not existing and lose your bet, you will suffer a major loss (missing heaven). If you bet on the Christian version of God's existing and it turns out to be wrong, your losses will be fairly minor: mainly having to experience a number of not very exciting Sunday mornings. Surely, Pascal suggests, it is in your interest to have religious faith. You can get it not through some effort of will but rather through acting as if you have it (going to church, taking the sacraments, etc.), which will in time result in your coming to believe what you had been only acting as if you believed.

Pascal's wager does contain at least two claims about human nature: that people by and large would prefer to go to heaven rather than miss out, and also that people's beliefs tend to be heavily influenced by the patterns of their lives. But these claims might seem fairly obvious. In some ways his most striking claim about human nature is a different one, focusing on how we spend our daily lives.

Normally any person could spend a sizable part of life by herself or himself and might well during that time think about the character of her or his life and how it could be made more meaningful. Pascal believed that a great many people don't want to pursue such thoughts. He observed that they often will go to great lengths to avoid the quiet periods in which they might occur.

Pascal suggested that the way in which many people avoid thinking about their lives is that they search for diversions, activities that will avoid the periods of reflection. Going to parties, running around with friends, hunting, and playing games all might seem to promote this end. As Pascal saw it, the more excitement these activities provide, the more we crave them.[2] If Pascal had imagined the invention of television (a supreme distraction), he would have been both fascinated and horrified.

This implicit claim about human nature can be put as follows. It is human nature to be inclined to be superficial and to avoid sustained thought about what is spiritually important. Pascal held that to be a human being was to occupy an awkward position midway between that of angels and that of brute animals. The angels (if one does not count those who fell with Satan) just naturally behave very well: they have no real moral or spiritual choices. Brute animals are unable to present to themselves moral or spiritual problems, so they too do not have any choices of these sorts that they have to make. In some sense they are lucky, compared to us.

We, as awkward in-between beings, do have extremely important choices in life, and what we choose (unlike what good angels choose) is hardly automatic. This is a real burden. It should not be surprising that we attempt to escape it through diversions.

This motivation is enhanced by the negative elements character-istic of much of human life. Pascal remarked, "As men are not able to cure death, wretchedness, ignorance, they have decided, in order to be happy, not to think about those things."[3] All the same, it is for our own good if we reject some of the diversions and spend more time thinking about the quality of our spiri-tual life.

Some readers may think both that there is some important truth in what Pascal said, and that it is not quite the whole truth of how a spiritually fulfilled human life can be constructed (or alternatively could be missed). Even if Pascal is right about the value of thinking seriously about the character of one's life—and even if he is also right in suggesting that many of us use diversions to avoid that thought—some activities that are a bit like diversions might have considerable value. One might nomi-nate those that involve close and caring relations with others or the sustained expression of valuable skills. Pascal might have conceded some of this, especially given his own work in mathematics.

Jean-Jacques Rousseau was an eighteenth-century thinker whose views in many respects are liberal. He regarded societies in which social class played a prominent role as in some sense unnatural and harmful to those who lived in them. His first major success was in a contest for the best answer to the ques-tion "Has the progress of the sciences and arts contributed to the corruption or to the improvement of human conduct?" He won with his *Discourse upon the Origin and Foundation of the Inequality among Mankind.*

Rousseau's main interests were in social and political policy, and he cannot be said to have had a full-fledged theory of human nature. He did have a positive, near-romanticist view of humans as they would have been in a state of nature, before the institutions of "civilized" society developed. Civilized soci-ety, it seemed to him, tends to undermine any harmony among distinct individuals. We can guard against this, in his view, by adhering to the general will, which might be thought of as pointing toward the common good.

This by itself tells us something, but perhaps not a great deal, about human nature. In his prize-winning essay, though, Rousseau had a sharp and telling insight into a human characteristic that might have developed as a byproduct of social inequality. He spoke of the "universal desire for reputation, honors, and preferences, which devours us all," and the general urge to be noticed, "making oneself the topic of conversation."[4]

That there is a general desire to be noticed and to be thought of as important is not a surprising idea, although—when we think about what people want most in life—it might not come close to the top of the list. All the same, anyone who is at home in the world of our time can regard what Rousseau said as obviously correct. Politicians and business executives are likely to want to be noticed as successful and to be thought of as people who make a difference. Authors, artists, and composers usually like to have their work mentioned and like even more for it to be experienced with some admiration. A simpleminded view of what most people want in life centers on pleasures and perhaps also on wealth (which does not always give much pleasure to the person who has it). But a broader view includes what Rousseau noted.

It may look as if the desire to be noticed and to be thought important can be regarded as just one variety of the desire for pleasures. It is true that many people who have such desires do think that being thought to be important, or being a celebrity, would give pleasure. But there is some evidence that people who come to be thought important, or become celebrities, often after a while dislike the experience.

Too much attention can be burdensome. Celebrities sometimes complain about lack of privacy or about eager strangers approaching them while saying meaningless things. One risk is of becoming someone's imaginary friend, or (as in the case of John Lennon) imaginary enemy. The writer J. D. Salinger was a well-known example of someone who retreated from celebrity, as did the actress Greta Garbo. Given all of this, some people might come to think that being seen as important would not in fact be pleasant, even if they (in one of the kinks that sometimes is part of people's natures) continue to desire it.

This points toward a larger subject: the frequent disconnect between what we desire and what we will or would find pleasant. It is arguable that to desire something is to think of it as pleasant or at least to find pleasant our idea of it. This might suggest that what is desired would in fact usually be pleasant. But common experience also suggests that you should be careful in what you wish for. Many hoped-for outcomes turn out to be disappointing. It may be that there is no general and reliable connection between desire and the pleasure that would result from fulfillment of the desire.

Notes

1. *The Bezels of Wisdom,* trans. R. W. J. Austin (New York: Paulist Press, 1980). A fuller discussion of this book than can be provided here is to be found in chapter 4 of my *Classic Asian Philosophy: A Guide to the Essential Texts,* 2nd ed. (New York: Oxford University Press, 2007).

2. See Pascal, *Pensées,* trans. Roger Ariew (Indianapolis: Hackett Publishing Co., 2005), pp. 38–43.

3. Ibid., p. 38.

4. Jean-Jacques Rousseau, *Discourse on the Origin of Inequality,* trans. Donald A. Cress (Indianapolis: Hackett Publishing Co., 1992), p. 67.

Questions for Further Consideration

1. Is Pascal's negative view of "diversions" justified? Aren't they the best safeguard against boredom? Or does the lack of higher purpose that diversions encourage outweigh boredom?

2. Is the idea that Spinoza and Ibn al-Arabi roughly share—that our nature has an inherent link with God—compatible with the fact that there appear to be evil and inadequate people?

Recommended Further Reading

Philosophical context for Ibn al-Arabi is provided by Peter Adamson and Richard C. Taylor, eds., *The Cambridge Companion to Arabic Philosophy* (Cambridge: Cambridge University Press, 2005). There is a chapter on Pascal in Frederick Copleston, *History of Philosophy,* vol. 4 (London: Burns Oates and Washbourne, 1960). A good book on Rousseau is N. J. H. Dent, *Rousseau* (Oxford: Blackwell, 1988).

Part IV

SOME CONCLUSIONS

Chapter 15

Human Nature in Philosophy
and in Everyday Thought

What the last twelve chapters have provided is a kaleidoscope of human nature rather than a single fixed and definite image. Should this be a disappointment? Or should we reconcile ourselves to the fact that philosophers almost always disagree, and then perhaps try to declare a winner?

Let me declare my own view—not of human nature but rather of the enterprise of formulating a theory of human nature. This is to reject two extreme (and I think untenable) sorts of positions. One is to insist that a worthwhile account of human nature must be definite and hold true of people at all times and in all social conditions. The other tempting extreme is to hold that there could not be such an account or anything even remotely like it. Human nature is various, and that is the last word on the subject.

Here is what seems to me to be a plausible intermediate sort of position. There are many different cultures that affect how human beings within them develop and behave. Also, any specific culture is likely not to be entirely changeless: styles of thought and behavior can change with time. Therefore it would be unreasonable to expect an account of human nature that is definite and holds true of people at all times and in all social conditions. It is not unreasonable, though, to think it possible to arrive at an account of human nature that is largely true. This would be an account that captured ways in which a great many people, in various cultures, tend to think and behave at most times. Perhaps there are a number of largely true accounts, each of them somewhat different from the others.

We can concede, in other words, that a plausible outcome of a search for human nature can be a kaleidoscope rather than a single true image. This is consistent with the claim that all, or almost all, of the images in the kaleidoscope have *some* truth to them. They do not add up to a simple and definite portrayal of human nature. But they can add up to a degree of enlightenment about what (in some aspects of life) we can repeatedly encounter or can expect.

Philosophy is not a science, and the sort of conclusion just described may well seem quite unscientific. It is worth bearing in mind, though, that there are many kinds of study which, by the same standards, are not scientific (or at least not entirely scientific) which still can lead to a sort of knowledge. These include many impressive historical, psychological, and sociological findings.

Here is one way of appreciating this possibility. What enables some scientific accounts to seem definitive is that they are precise. Precision requires one or both of two things. Either the distinctions among the things studied have to be sharp and entirely clear or the realities studied can be reported in numerical terms. Physics in particular yields some precise and definitive results that are made possible by its use of mathematics.

History and the social sciences do admit of findings that can be expressed numerically and seem definitive. This includes the numbers of people recorded as voting in certain ways on an issue, or consumer prices, or dates. It appears to be a definitive truth that Columbus reached the New World in 1492. However, definitive truths of this sort float on the surface of history and the social sciences. At a deeper level there can be investigations of motivations, interactions, and causal patterns.

The most important point is this. Much that is concluded by historians and social scientists is not straightforwardly definitive. There can be a variety of very good accounts of (for example) the causes of the French Revolution or of the psychology of wishing to withdraw from one's society. In each case, perhaps at some times, one of them might be considered tentatively "definitive"—with the qualification that it is very unlikely to prove to be the last word. Other attractive accounts may appear.

This is less of a live possibility for claims in which numbers play a crucial role. Social scientists can report accurately the percentage, among a group of respondents, of those who on questionnaires rate their happiness at a certain level. This will amount to the truth, and the whole truth, about the percentage in this particular group of respondents. But it gives us only a rather rough idea of the deeper matter of how happy they in fact are.

In a paper on this topic, I have contrasted accounts that give us, as it were, the whole and final truth, with those that do not but which we reasonably could judge to be "objective."[1] Some accounts of the causes of the French Revolution may be biased or one-sided or may fail entirely to deal with important factors. We would deny that these are objective. Others may be balanced, unbiased, and reasonably good in dealing with all major factors, while hardly being the last word on the subject. Perhaps there never will be a last word on the subject. In any case, there can be good, "objective" accounts that differ from one another, and that cannot simply be dismissed.

My suggestion is that theories of human nature are like what has just been characterized, at least in two respects. One is that no theory yields a final and definitive truth. The other is that there can be good accounts of human nature that cannot simply be dismissed. Even if they are not the last word on the subject and are not entirely true, they can be largely true, capturing (as the good, "objective" historical accounts do) a significant part of the subject.

What It Is for a Theory of Human
Nature to Be Largely True

Any theory of human nature will have to be about how people think and behave. My suggestion has been that it would be unreasonable to expect to discover that there are some respects in which everyone—always—thinks or behaves in the same way. A good deal of psychological research points in the same direction. It is not very common to find a study whose conclusion is that in circumstances X all subjects will do Y. There are, on the other hand, a number of important and indeed revelatory studies in which it turned out that most (or perhaps almost all) subjects behaved in a certain way.

Given this, we can see that studies of human thought and behavior can vary in how common what they describe is said to be. At the low end of this range are claims that occasionally human beings do (or think) X. Such claims should not be scorned: they can be very enlightening, especially if X is something that we find surprising in anyone. If X is unusual and surprising, such a study could be used to argue that human nature is more elastic or variable than most of us have been inclined to think.

All of the theories of human nature presented in this book are higher up in the range of claims about human thought or behavior. That is, what they describe is claimed to be common and not uncommon. In this respect, what they claim is comparable to the psychological findings already referred to.

There are two further complications that we need to bear in mind. One is that some of the theories presented are keyed not so much to the actual thought and behavior of a large number of people but rather to what is maintained would be conducive to a fulfilled life, possibly for a large number of people. The Indian and Chinese philosophical accounts presented in the first part of the book have that quality, pointing toward what amounts to a desirable second nature in life. Value judgments clearly have a role in this unlike what they have in some other (more matter of fact) theories of human nature, such as Thomas Hobbes'.

The other complication is that the theories clearly are not intended to provide a comprehensive overview of all of human behavior and thought. Rather the attempt is to focus on an important element of human thought and behavior and to claim that this is universal or near-universal. Hobbes' account of human appetitive and competitive behavior has this quality, as does Aristotle's claim that man is the rational animal.

Once we see that each of these accounts is designed to apply to one or two elements in human life and also that they focus on different elements, there is an obvious thought: two very different theories both could be to a large extent right. Perhaps this could be extended to all of the theories of human nature that have been presented. That is, it might turn out that they all are to a large extent right.

There are a number of reasons why, even if such a claim seems plausible, one needs to be cautious. Any theory of human nature can be taken to apply not only to living human beings but also to human life in the past and in the future. Perhaps there is a reasonable cutoff point in relation to the past? It is not clear that if Aristotle had somehow known about cavemen and cavewomen he would have severely modified his view of human nature. He might well have insisted that the cavepeople were not full-fledged human beings and that his theory did not apply to them.

It is hard to know what to say about the future, other than that it will not be finished any time soon. We can imagine only in a very sketchy way scenarios that might seem optimistic or extremely pessimistic. In a future human society on other planets, it imaginably might be that virtually no one has the appetitive and competitive characteristics pointed to by Hobbes' theory. On a future planet Earth on which global warming has reached its maximum and devastating effect, it imaginably might be that relatively few humans are more rational than cavemen and cavewomen.

This suggests, at the least, that theories of human nature keyed to facts of how human beings live have to be taken with qualifications such as "up to now" or "unless something radically changes." In the remainder of this chapter, we will assume such qualifications. Let me add that this is how remarks about what is "human nature" are normally taken in everyday discourse. They are regarded as offering a view of the kinds of thought and behavior that we often can expect of people—because they are human beings.

Questions remain about the ways in which a number of quite diverse theories could be held all to be largely true. These will be taken up in the next section.

Theories as Largely True, but Not a Final and Definitive Truth

The previous remarks suggest that a promising theory of human nature could not, somehow, turn out to be a final and definitive truth. This is because of two factors. One is the influence of particular cultures. The other is the pervasiveness in human history of change.

It was suggested, though, that there might be considerable truth to all of the theories of human nature presented in this book (different though they are), with the implicit qualifications of "up to now" and "unless something radically changes." To develop this case will require meeting an obvious objection. What about theories that seem to conflict with each other?

Do some of the theories surveyed actually conflict with one another? Any response must begin by dividing theories into two groups. One group would include theories that claim the nature of human life is such that it needs certain features in order to be fulfilled. The Asian theories first surveyed clearly fall within this group, and a case can be made for including Plato's and Aristotle's theories.

Plato's and Aristotle's accounts, however, have features that can be held to place them within a second group: theories that describe human life as it generally is. Hobbes' theory of human nature is an example of this, as is the theory that can be associated with the doctrine of original sin. Aristotle's view that humans are the rational animals also might seem to belong with these, but perhaps not so simply. The cultivation of rationality also was thought by Aristotle to be essential to human fulfillment.

Two theories in the first group might seem to conflict if each ,in effect recommends a path to fulfillment that would be rejected by the other. By this standard, each of the Indian or Chinese theories does conflict with the others. That said, the conflict is not entirely sharp. The Indian and the Daoist accounts share an emphasis on increasing detachment, with resultant serenity. Confucius and his followers certainly do not recommend the same kind of detachment, but Confucius does make it clear that an appropriate valuing of "internal" goods can lead to a degree of detachment and serenity.

There is a further complication. Many of us to some degree compartmentalize our lives and tend to behave differently in some contexts from the way we normally behave in others. Often there is a real division between one's professional or public life and one's private life. This suggests the possibility that elements of two very different views of human fulfillment could be combined in the same life.

A specific example is the different views of human fulfillment contained in Confucianism and in Daoism. The great historian of Chinese philosophy Fung Yu-lan remarked that after a certain time versions of Confucianism and Daoism tended to complement each other, which suggests that they might be combined in some lives.[2] Confucianism might seem especially suited for public life and Daoism for private life.

There certainly are great differences within the group of theories that primarily focus on the nature of human life as it actually is. To what degree do these necessarily involve conflicts? Perhaps in some cases the degree is small. That two theories are different does not by itself point to anything like sharp conflict. They could both be focusing on elements that are common in human life and that indeed could be combined in one person's life.

There is one case in the second group of theories that looks like a clear conflict and was taken as such by some of the philosophers. This is the relation between the view of human nature advanced by Butler and by Hume and the prior view of Hobbes. Butler and Hume clearly took themselves to be arguing against Hobbes. It is easy to think that they cannot all be right.

The differences, however, when looked at carefully, are somewhat subtle. Neither Butler nor Hume, it seems to me, denied that human beings normally will have a streak of appetitive and competitive behavior. The difference on this point between them and Hobbes looks like one of emphasis. Hobbes treated the appetitive and competitive as central and important; Butler and Hume did not, but also did not deny that it is there within most of us.

Butler and Hume conversely emphasized the role in human life of sympathy and benevolence and of helpful and cooperative behavior. Did Hobbes flatly deny this? It might seem that by implication he did, in that leaving such factors out of his account is a statement of sorts. But we can imagine that Hobbes, if he had been confronted with instances of kind and disinterested behavior, would have admitted that such things happen, while denying that they are as common as we might like to think. The differences, again, could turn out to be matters of emphasis.

Other differences among the theories of human nature presented in this book can be regarded as matters of emphasis. It is possible—let me suggest—to be sympathetic to all of the theories (including the ones that focus mainly on the nature of a fulfilled life), and think again and again "there is something to this." How much truth (or appeal) each theory has will remain, of course, a matter for individual judgment.

Notes

1. "Precision in History," *Mind* 84 (1975): 374–389.

2. See *A Short History of Chinese Philosophy*, trans. Derk Bodde (New York: Free Press, 1948), p. 22.

Index

Adler, Alfred, 166
al-Arabi, Ibn, 29, 177–78
alienation, 143ff.
altruism, 114–15, 117
Anselm, 181
Anscombe, G. E. M., 140
a priori, 126–27, 139
Aquinas, Thomas, 29, 81, 181
Arendt, Hannah, viii, 11, 23,
    50, 169–76
Argyle, Michael, 53–54, 57,
    122
Aristotle, viii, 7–8, 13, 18, 50,
    52, 59ff., 81, 130, 132–34,
    171–72, 174, 193–95
Austen, Jane, 147

Barnes, Hazel, 166
Baudelaire, Charles, 162
benevolence, 5, 13, 20, 73–78,
    83, 103, 119–22
Bentham, Jeremy, 45, 114
Berlin, Isaiah, 153
Bible, 29, 43, 87, 89, 131, 178
Bodhisattva, 40
Boswell, James, 119, 123
Brandt, Richard, 115, 122
Buddha, 6, 18, 27, 32, 43, 36ff.
Butler, Bishop Joseph, 8,
    10–11, 21, 32, 37, 81, 103,
    105, 113, 115–18, 196

Calvin, John, 29

Chuang-Tzu (a.k.a., Zhuangzi),
    91
class divisions, 150ff.
compassion, 38–39, 63
Confucius, viii, 4, 5, 7, 15, 19,
    23, 27, 43–57, 59, 66, 73, 76,
    79, 84, 132–33, 195
Csikszentmihalyi, Mihaly, 54,
    57

Daoism, 5, 14, 65–66, 195
Darwin, 107ff.
Dennett, Daniel, 109, 110
Descartes, René, 126, 181
desire, 37–39, 41, 67, 121,
    184–85
despair, 157
determinism, 163–64
Dickens, Charles, 108
distinctness, 169ff.
division of labor, 148ff.

Eddington, Arthur, 35
Ekman, Paul, 23
Ellington, James, 140
existential choice, 161
existentialism, 156
existentialist psychoanalysis,
    165–66

faith, 156ff.
fear of heights, 158–59

197

Also Available from Hackett Publishing Company

Suzanne Cunningham, *What is a Mind? An Integrative Introduction to the Philosophy of Mind*

The Good Life, edited, with Introduction, by Charles Guignon

Philip J. Ivanhoe, *Confucian Moral Self Cultivation,* second edition

Joel J. Kupperman, *Six Myths about the Good Life: Thinking about What Has Value*

John Perry, *Dialogue on Personal Identity and Immortality*

John Perry, *Identity, Personal Identity, and The Self*